UNDERSTANDING
RELATIONSHIP

UNDERSTANDING RELATIONSHIP

The Relating Self · Synastry · Compository

SUZANNE ROUGH

authorHOUSE®

AuthorHouse™ UK Ltd.
1663 Liberty Drive
Bloomington, IN 47403 USA
www.authorhouse.co.uk
Phone: 0800.197.4150

Published by AuthorHouse 06/17/2014

ISBN: 978-1-4969-8258-2 (sc)
ISBN: 978-1-4969-8259-9 (e)

Library of Congress Control Number: 2014910192

Other Astrological Works by Suzanne Rough

Understanding the Natal Chart – An Esoteric Approach to Learning Horoscopy
Working with Time: Recognising and Using Opportunity
Transitional Astrology – Giving an Esoteric Role to Orthodox Astrology

To Chris, Sandy, and Elizabeth – friends for all seasons.

Contents

Preface

I wrote this work at the beginning of the 2000s. Behind me were fifteen colourful years as a professional astrologer, working on the New Age centre circuit whilst – in the United Kingdom, at least – the New Age was in full flower.

Those years, for all the extravagance, indulgence, and self-dramatisation, remain in memory as the most enjoyable of my working life. But nothing stands still. By the time I began work on this book, the excitement and sense of destiny which had inspired large numbers of us to upturn our lives was dying down, and many were counting the cost in terms of the relationships they had lost.

It was long-term, established relationships which were most obviously and adversely affected. This was often a source of hurt and bewilderment to those who had lost their partners and, in some cases, their family because they had 'chosen a spiritual path'. That was the perception, anyway.

Each year at that time, I was giving a couple hundred in-depth readings. Nearly every one of my clients wanted to know how to think about the fact that things were going wrong in their relationship lives, when they themselves were trying to doing the right thing by developing themselves spiritually.

This work is an attempt made by an astrologer, not a therapist, to open out the matter of relationship and create for it a context that is suitable for people who, in committing to spirituality, have committed to change. I do not need to damage to anyone's belief in reincarnation to remark that, as a tool of explanation, it is not very helpful so long as it is focused on who was who and who did what to whom. It is the quality of the memory in the psyche that we have to deal with, because it is this which is shaping our lives and relationships. We can acknowledge the role of the past without engaging in the personality drama.

This is a book written for astrology students with a working knowledge of horoscopy – and for practitioners.

The changes which I have made in this revised edition are mostly to remove observations that were made for the benefit of my students of an earlier time. They do not have the same relevance now.

Suzanne Rough
April 2014

Introduction: Understanding Relationship

Beyond question, personal relationships are responsible for bringing more Westerners to astrology than any other matter. Whether these people come as students or as clients, their motivation is usually the same: a desire to understand more fully the situation in which they find themselves. The fact that they (or, perhaps, it is time to say *we*) should turn to astrology in such circumstances is an acknowledgement – on some level, at least – that there may be more at issue here than simply having or not having who and what we want and think we should have.

Other matters simply do not have the same piquancy. We may be drawn to astrology for a range of reasons, but the fact remains that, likely as not, it will be a relationship situation that provides the incentive for us to make the first phone call, send the first email, or attend the first class that will actually take us into the world of astrology.

This is why problematic relationship situations represent such an important opportunity to develop a different understanding of life. If we are prepared to consider that relationships have a developmental function, then we may be able to understand that our close personal relationships challenge the self-centredness which limits us spiritually. Relationships require more of us than merely our own views about how things should be.

The source of so much suffering and limitation in relationship is, often, our own inadequate expectations. We hold onto ideas about how things should be, often without examining where these assumptions have come from or whether they serve us, and we go through hell when the outcome does not conform to our expectations. Our suffering may not be caused by the nature of the situation at all, but by the fact that it departs from our expectation of how it should be.

Usually, people who are interested in spirituality readily accept the idea that they will be challenged in the interests of their development, complete with the notion that their personal relationships are the means by which they are most seriously challenged. So often, however, people fail to hold onto this understanding when confronted with a challenging situation in their own lives that is producing a profound emotional reaction. This is what it means to be human, as most of us are only too aware.

Few of us are accepting of difficulties in our personal relationships. We view them as a sign that things have 'gone wrong', because conflict is out of place in a situation that we expect to be loving and harmonious.

The astrologer does not see things gone wrong; the astrologer sees things working out in the only way they can, for as long as a certain kind of situation and a certain kind of awareness come together.

Astrology cannot fix the conflict, but it can attempt to explain what is going on and why. Because of this, then, we have a better chance of finding a different way of proceeding with our lives and our relationships.

It is not disappointment and sadness caused by having unfulfilled hopes that ruins lives. In time, we can usually recover from those. What ruins lives is the distrust, anger, and bitterness caused by the belief that what has occurred is in some way aberrant and purposeless. These emotions are toxins and distort our way of looking at life. Eventually, by some or other means, Pluto will have to clear them out of our emotional body.

In times of change – and all times are times of change for those who have truly committed to spirituality – we need a different perspective and different expectations from those which regulated the lives of our parents and grandparents. Love has work to do in our world. It must be allowed to change the way its expresses itself in our lives.

The twelfth-century Sufi mystic Jelaluddin Rumi taught that relationship is made up not of two, but of three, components: self, other, and the relationship itself.

In this work, this idea is adopted and enlarged.

- The Individuals – Technique/Concept: The Relating Self
- Self and Other – Technique: Synastry
- The Relationship Itself – Technique: Compository

By these means, we look at relationship in a way that places it in the present, in the lives of people who want to use the opportunities that this time is bringing us.

Chapter 1

Opening Out the Matter of Relationship

1. Some Philosophical Considerations

The ideas offered in this chapter are designed to open out thinking about relationship, a matter which is so often enclosed in assumption. The ability to use the techniques described in this book does not depend upon the acceptance of these ideas, but the ideas may help provide a context in which to look afresh at the matter of relationship.

Very few of us, no matter how spiritually aware, see a challenging relationship situation as a positive experience, not when we meet it in our own lives. We want our intimate relationships to be only smooth and happy. This is more than a desire; it is a belief that anything other than a smooth and happy relationship is aberrant. A practicing astrologer has to be prepared for this and know how to steer the reading through the minefield of expectation and assumption in order to give clients something new and valuable to think about that might help their situation.

Personal Reality

For the esotericist, material existence is a process of disclosure. For a human being, life on Earth is an opportunity to explore the awareness that we have brought with us into incarnation. If we are given a present that is wrapped, we have to open it in order to know what is inside. And so it is with what we have brought into incarnation and so readily call *ourselves,* without having much understanding of ourselves at all. To know what we contain, we have to get it out and look at it.

This is what our time on Earth does for us: it allows what is within us to be unpacked and revealed through our relationship with all the things that we perceive to be outside ourselves: other people, animals, nature, ideas, and situations. This way, we find the truth about ourselves.

Of course, we may not see the truth because we may not be looking. Indeed, we may be taking very good care not to look, precisely because we do not want to see anything that might challenge the way of seeing ourselves and our lives with which we have become familiar. But for those who want to find the truth about themselves, it is made possible by a process of objectification, which uses the material world as a reflecting surface.

We will manifest situations in accordance with the design of our personalities, and we will experience those situations in accordance with our level of understanding. This is what it means to have a personal reality.

The esotericist does not have an opinion about this: it is what it is. A personal reality is a means of functioning in the material world, but it is also a source of limitation, because all personal realities exclude. They are like a bubble, enclosing the individual within his or her way of looking at the world ('I'm all right. It's everyone else who is the problem!'). It is the task of spirituality to loosen our grip so that we become more inclusive in our way of looking at life – and more open to possibility.

Conditioning is part of the process of building a personal reality. Whether familial or social, conditioning helps us to build an identity; but that conditioned identity will eventually become a limitation because it encourages us to pushes away other in order to define self in a certain way. This is when the challenges begin: when, with a part of ourselves, we attract an experience that challenges the part that holds the idea of how things should be.

People who are consciously working on self are hoping to free themselves from the limitations in the form of conditioned reactions. We will examine very closely what is thrown back by the mirror of daily life, especially when it bears the stamp of the Moon and Saturn. This way, we stand to come to a better level of self-understanding and increase our opportunity to get free from the patterns that keep us in repetition. This is the province of psychology and psychological astrology (see endnote 1).

For the esoteric astrologer who is concerned with the holistic view – with all that we might be, not just what we are – these things are true:

- The part that attracts the new is our true identity in this lifetime. It is represented by the Sun and is backed up by Uranus, which is the ambassador of the soul.
- The conditioned part of self that holds the idea of how things should be is represented by the Moon and Saturn. They attract their own kind of experiences, and they are familiar to us.

Out of incarnation, awareness does not have the same opportunity to understand itself because it has no objectivity. Therefore, it is in a non-comparative state. If awareness is dominated by suffering, then it has no scope to understand itself any better. This is why suicide is a such tragedy. For as long as we are in incarnation, we have the opportunity to understand ourselves better through our relationships with things, animate and inanimate, and to learn to handle things better.

Ouspensky, the Russian esotericist, said, 'When three forces meet together things happen. If they do not come together, nothing happens.' (see endnote 2)

Three forces come together when we are in incarnation:

- Life: the opportunity
- Quality: our true selves or essence
- Appearance: manifestation

What it is able to happen, then, are shifts in consciousness, great or small, depending on our willingness to cooperate with the process. And cooperation starts with respect for the opportunity and a regard for time, which, for all of us in the material world, is limited.

Personal Relationships

Our personal relationships disclose our emotional selves, showing us what we desire, what we fear, and what our hopes and expectations are.

Master D.K. says, 'As a man thinks *in his heart,* so he is.' Our experiences in our personal relationships, whether with partners, friends, parents, or children, influence thinking in the heart in a very direct way. Our relationships offer us the best opportunities to control and refine selfishness and greed and to open up to positive emotion and find more room in the sealed bubble that is personal reality.

When we are aware of this, we can understand why it is that our personal relationships are so important – and why they touch us so deeply. They are spiritual opportunities and require much of us in the form of new awareness.

The Composition of Human Personality

Body Chakra, or Energy Centre

Mental

- higher mental/spiritual
- lower mental/intellectual
- head centres
- throat

Astral

- higher emotional
- heart

- lower/desire
- solar plexus

Physical

- etheric
- dense
- sacral
- base

Our Emotional Selves

Esoteric tradition attributes seven sub-planes to each plane of nature. This is a useful concept for understanding the human emotional body. It presents it as having seven 'settings', or levels, not all of which may be accessible to us. The higher settings may remain like sealed rooms.

The craving for material things and physical sensation, regardless of the cost to others, represents the lowest level of our range of emotions. At the highest level is the aspiration to merge with something greater than self. This aspiration enables us to transcend selfish impulses, making us able to respond to things in and of themselves, not in a way that presupposes what they might mean to us. This way, we are freed from the tyranny of self-centredness.

Our relationships are our vehicle for travelling the spectrum of emotional states. Psychic sensitivity and intuition are both faculties that use emotional energy and that increase as we respond to higher emotional states.

- highly evolved man/woman – heart centre fully open/brow centre open/intuition functioning
- spiritual aspirant – solar plexus active but heart centre beginning to open/psychically sensitive
- undeveloped man/woman – solar plexus very active and heart centre not yet open/some erratic, low-level psychic capacity

Venus works within this spectrum, making us appreciate certain qualities in other people and other things. Mars supplies passion and raw energy; Jupiter, positivity; and Saturn, sobriety and realism in accordance with how our personal reality understands those things. Uranus provides opportunities to break with old patterns; Neptune provides insight into what it would be like to be free of our separatist tendencies. Pluto exposes what lies beneath the surface, including the things that are active beneath the surface of consciousness and that may be driving us unnoticed.

All these planetary principles express themselves through people and animals, bringing into our lives parents, children, relatives, friends, partners, pets, and teachers who express these things and arouse reactions in us. We, in turn, embody these energies for others.

The Past

The past lives on in our emotional patterns. A major area of conflict in most of our lives is between the head and the heart. The heart indicates what we desire based on our emotional selves. The head provides a more holistic assessment of our lives and the opportunities open to us, telling us what would be more appropriate and what would enable us to refine our emotional bodies.

Our relationships are called up by a particular aspect of our emotional selves. For some people, it is the desire for emotional security that drives them in a relationship; for others, it may be the desire for freedom, and so on. Depending upon the pattern, the relationships we attract may support that desire or may challenge it. The relationship may fit well into the overall direction of our life, or it may create imbalance.

All choices that are informed by our emotions have to answer eventually to that more holistic view. The more aware we become, the more in touch we are with the holistic view, and the more this view challenges the choices of the emotional self. This is why choosing a spiritual path rarely makes our experience of existing relationships any easier – if our emotional selves are still choosing what is familiar, whilst our heads are choosing development, and signing up for change. It is from this conflict that so much suffering arises. It is like playing a cassette while simultaneously pressing fast forward and rewind.

To hold onto the idea that certain areas of our lives should be free from challenge and change is to make things difficult for ourselves. There are no such areas, least of all the area of personal relationships. The problem here is in our thinking and expectations, and our unrealistic hope that we bring to bear: that all we have to do is meet the right person and let love sort out the rest. From the standpoint of spiritual development, the great love affairs of literature and the silver screen are mostly dysfunctional and psychotic. Considering how they influence expectation, this should be food for thought!

The more we understand about our relating selves, the better able we are to understand the relationships we attract. The esotericist knows that whilst opposites attract on the physical level, like attracts like on the emotional level.

Causation

To the esotericist, any kind of blame, whether of people or circumstances, is insupportable. It is our own patterns that are responsible for what we attract to us: a parent, partner, or child who is simply externalising the principles and patterns that exist in our own psyche.

The causes were put in place long ago in human evolution. We all have a share of the past with which to deal before we can eventually bring the areas of conflict in the collective psyche into harmony. We bring our share from the common stockpot into our incarnation. For the purposes of our lifetime, the content of our psyches is 'ours', giving us our sense of familiarity with certain kinds of people and situations. Re-engaging, the meeting of the old and the new, will give rise to fresh new reactions in the consciousness of the personality. These will have to be processed, too.

Through a natal chart, using certain tools and techniques, astrologers can see the conflict between past and present very clearly. This disclosure will not lessen the conflict, but recognising a truth may raise the situation to a level above blame, reproach, and resentment, which is good place from which to look afresh at our lives.

2. Case Study: Hannah and Mark

Hannah and Mark, our subjects for the purposes of this course, live in the town (Brighton, UK) where they were born. They met when they were young teenagers, at a time when Hannah was going through turmoil in her relationship with her mother. Since her mother and father's divorce, Hannah had lived with her mother and younger brother. When her mother remarried, Hannah did not like it. She felt as though she had been pushed aside. So, she went to live with her father, visiting her mother only occasionally.

Meanwhile, Mark's father and mother were divorcing. He, his father, and his little brother came to live in a house a few doors away from Hannah's mother.

Hannah and Mark met when Hannah visited her mother in the summer of her fourteenth year (Mark's fifteenth). They have been together ever since. They are now in their early twenties.

They are a strikingly handsome couple, but it is their companionability that is most impressive. Hannah, who was rather sullen as a child and was inclined to fall out with her girlfriends, is always chatting animatedly to Mark. He listens as though what he is hearing is fascinating. They never appear out of sorts with each other. They now have their own flat in a different part of town, but they visit Hannah's mother and Mark's father often. Mark and his father go running together. They are both ranked quite high in the county league.

Since Hannah's mother and her new husband separated, Hannah and Mark spend the weekends with her in her house so that she does not feel lonely.

All three go out shopping on Saturdays, which is a social ritual amongst their friends and families. Mark and Hannah talk together whilst Hannah's mother is lost in her own thoughts.

On Monday mornings, the couple leave early to go back to their own flat before going into work. (Both passed on going to college.) They walk down the road at 6:30, chatting cheerfully and quite unhurried, regardless of the weather.

Together, they appear to occupy a different time and space, seeming utterly content with each other and with life. They have been this way for seven years now.

We will examine the charts of these two and the synastry between them, looking at whether this extraordinary companionship formed at a time of emotional difficulty, before either of them had much experience of other relationships, has room for growth.

Hannah
6 April 1983 / 03:15 BST / Brighton, England
Geocentric, Tropical, Koch House System
© Winstar Matrix Software

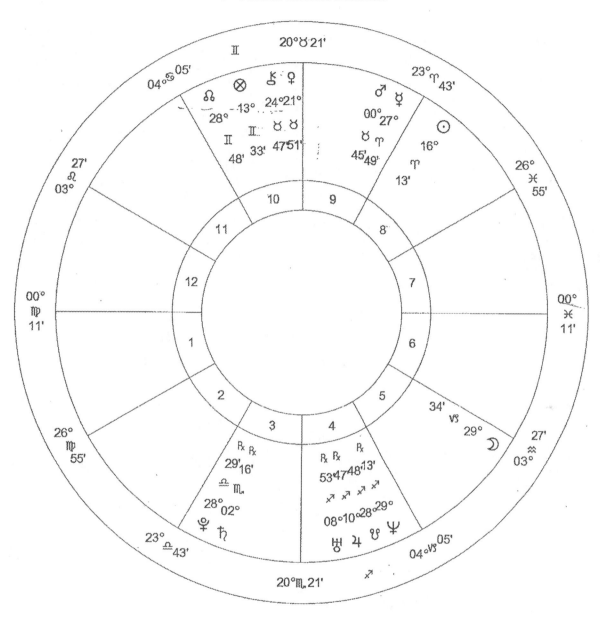

Mark
9 January 1982 / 12:19 GMT / Brighton, England
Geocentric, Tropical, Koch House System
© Winstar Matrix Software

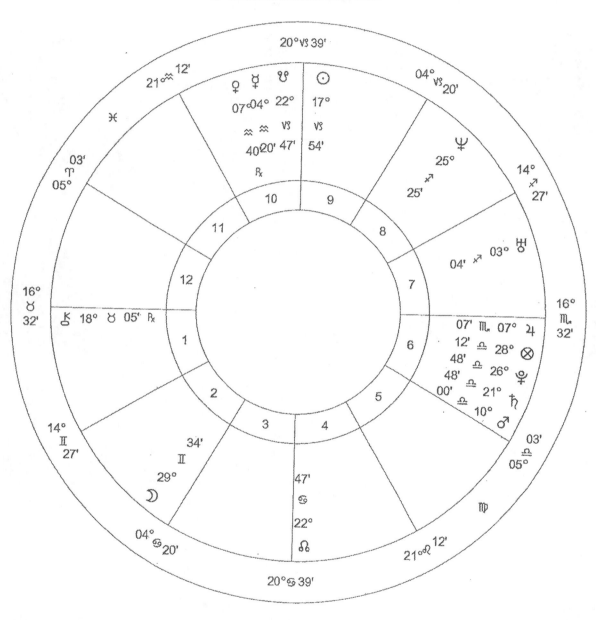

Endnote

1. In this context, I unreservedly recommend the works of the Jungian analysts–astrologers Liz Greene, Steven Arroyo, and Howard Sasportas.
2. *In Search of the Miraculous*; RKP, 1950

Part One

The Relating Self

Chapter 2

Finding the Relating Self in the Natal Chart
– General Considerations

Introduction

The Techniques of Orthodox Astrology

When it comes to applying astrology to the circumstances of everyday life, the perspectives of esoteric astrology are supplementary to those of orthodox astrology, which has grown up in response to questions arising about personality. So many of those questions have arisen out of relating situations.

In India, demand for charts to identify suitable marriage partners has been a major factor in keeping Hindu astrology a part of modern Indian life. In the West, amongst people who are accepting of astrology, synastry and, to a lesser extent, compository are popular branches of the discipline. Although they belong to orthodox astrology, these techniques can be made more useful as developmental tools by applying an esoteric perspective. Indeed, the same may be said of almost any technique known to orthodox astrology. Astrology is simply a language that must be organised to suit the situations to which it is being applied. For example, a person who has no interest in spirituality is unlikely to want a synastric report that focuses on the developmental purpose of the relationship, preferring instead one that emphasizes compatibility, or the lack thereof, on a personality level. The same *techniques* will serve different kinds of interests and motivation; it is the quality of the considerations employed by the astrologer who is using the techniques that will make the difference.

The Effects of Time

As any astrology student who has worked with time will appreciate, the natal chart is a still of a moment captured from the ceaseless flow that is life. We use special time-working techniques (see endnote 1) to capture the effects brought about by time. These will show that the house cusps are advancing, as are the planets within the houses.

This means that throughout the life, different decanates and different signs will appear on the house cusps (identified below) as having special importance in understanding relationships. Also, different planets will appear in these key houses.

The influence of all changes should be assessed and viewed as an overlay on the original pattern, one that has relevance to the present time.

1. The Houses

First, let us remind ourselves of the area of life ruled by each house.

- First house: self/self-assertion; natural ruler: Mars
- Second house: values/possessions; natural ruler: Venus
- Third house: communication/education/environment; natural ruler: Mercury
- Fourth house: past/home/mother; natural ruler: Moon
- Fifth house: creativity and individuality; natural ruler: Sun
- Sixth house: vocation/physical body/health; natural ruler: Mercury
- Seventh house: structured relationships of all kinds; natural ruler: Venus
- Eighth house: emotional attachments/union with others; natural rulers: Mars and Pluto
- Ninth house: spiritual quest; natural ruler: Jupiter
- Tenth house: career/lifestyle/aspirations; natural ruler: Saturn
- Eleventh house: fellowship/friendship/ideals; natural rulers: Saturn and Uranus
- Twelfth house: retreat from the world/union with the divine; natural rulers: Jupiter and Neptune

The Key Houses of the Relating Self

The Ascendant and Descendant are the cusps of the first and seventh houses, respectively. This axis is the principal key to our personal relationships. But there are other axes which are also revealing of our relating selves:

- second–eighth: reveals the desire nature
- fifth–eleventh: reveals the relationship that, as individuals, we will have to the group

These cusps represent thresholds of areas of the chart that enable us to see into our relating selves.

A. The Ascendant–Descendant Axis: What We Are

The Ascendant is the cusp of the House of Aries, and its natural ruler is Mars. This is the House of the Self. The Descendant is the cusp of the House of Libra, the House of Relationships. Its natural ruler is Venus.

In a natal chart, the Ascendant–Descendant axis describes the quality of being that we will express more or less consciously throughout life. The signs on these two hyleg points will be, of course, polarities.

Whilst the sign of the Ascendant indicates qualities that our upbringing will have encouraged us to demonstrate, at no matter how low a level (see endnote 2), the sign on the Descendant indicates qualities that are *unrecognised aspects of our own being.* These we have to meet 'on the outside', as expressed through others. In drawing close to others and in responding to the attraction of opposites, we are seeking for the missing part of ourselves. Plato called this impulse 'the desire and pursuit of the whole'.

Making a unity out of the two polarities is the point of our relationships, reflecting as it does the alignment of the personality and the soul.

The sign of the Ascendant indicates the qualities within us that we express readily and that, consciously or unconsciously, we are seeking to balance out by an encounter with the opposite. This may have a gender element, but the attraction transcends gender. If we examine the charts of relationships of significance – partners, parents, friends – it is not at all uncommon to find that the sign on the Ascendant of our own chart is the sign on the Descendant of the charts of the people close to us.

The sign on the Ascendant indicates the energy that people experience and to which they respond when they meet us. Our handshake will express those qualities (see endnote 3).

- the fire signs have warm hands
- the air signs have cool, soft hands
- the earth signs have cold, dry hands
- the water signs have cold, damp hands

B. The Second–Eighth Axis: What We Desire

H2 is the House of Values, which is the House of Taurus ruled by Venus. The sign on the cusp of H2 indicates what we desire, what drives us, and what we are happy to be seen pursuing.

The other end of the axis is the cusp of H8, the House of Scorpio, which is ruled by Pluto and which indicates the qualities with which others impress our desired nature. It also indicates what we want from others. We have a longing for what is missing from our lives and for the people who express the energy of the sign on the cusp of this house. We do not perceive ourselves as able to provide this energy for ourselves.

C. The Fifth–Eleventh Axis: With What We Align Ourselves

The fifth–eleventh axis pertains to individuality and to the individual's relationship to the group. H5 is the House of Leo, ruled by the Sun. H11 is the House of Aquarius, ruled by Uranus.

This axis is very important in determining the nature of a person's contribution to a relationship. The sign on the cusp of H5 indicates the optimum expression of a person's creative capacity, and the sign on the cusp of H11 indicates the quality of the group that will provide a suitable setting for this contribution.

As we commence this section on the planets, let us round them up and look at them from the point of view of relating activity. In this section, we will use two astrological terms in connection with the planets: natural and accidental.

- Natural rulers are those which rule the house according to the basic zodiacal arrangement, e.g. Mars rules House 1, House of Aries; Venus rules House 2, House of Taurus; etc.
- Accidental rulers are those which govern the sign on the house in a birth chart, which is determined by the time of birth and is subject to the effects of time.

The two luminaries, the Sun and the Moon, represent the following:

Present
Sun – present identity

Past
Moon – old idea of self

The planets represent the following:

Connecting:
Mercury
Venus

Asserting:
Mars

Expanding:
Jupiter

Structuring:
Saturn

Liberating:
Uranus

Transfiguring:
Neptune

Transforming:
Chiron
Pluto

- The houses that accommodate the inner planets indicate areas of life in which we are invited to function confidently.

- The houses occupied by the outer planets – which, in their different way, are all banishing principles – indicate that there is a development need to shift the focus from this area of life that has now served the purposes of the personality.
- If inner and outer planets appear together in the same house, then we are required to cooperate consciously with the matter of changing our approach and attitude in the area of life. Saturn, the Moon, and the south node will provide the clues as to the quality of the consciousness that is needed to undergo change.

The Luminaries and Planets as Significators

When they occupy or transit any of the four key relationship houses, planets will have a marked effect upon the unfolding of our relationship:

- The luminaries and inner and superior planets will draw our attention and energy into those areas of life.
- The involvement of the outer planets will override the personality's wishes and intention in order to free us from excessive reliance upon certain aspects of relating. Although its effects may be more subtle than those of the other outer planets, Neptune still challenges the personality by making it relax its defences.

Regardless of the houses that they rule accidentally, Venus (seventh house), Sun (fifth house), Mars and Pluto (eighth house), and Saturn and Uranus (eleventh house) will always be the natural rulers of the key relationship houses. Wherever they are in the natal chart, they are communicating back to the houses they rule and therefore have significance to the relating self.

The Sun

- Natural ruler of the fifth house
- By sign and house position, the Sun describes the true identity in this lifetime

The perception of self created by this placement of the Sun will supervise the planets as they manifest experiences, which, in turn, generate new ways of understanding how we should use our lifetime.

The Moon

- Natural ruler of the fourth house
- By sign and house position, the Moon describes an old idea of self held in past life, which is now a source of unquestioned assumption when it comes to what the self needs (and wants) in order to protect and preserve itself

In popular astrology, the Moon is associated with procreation and one's emotional states. To the esoteric astrologer, it is this and more: the Moon represents perpetuation. Physically, this means that we must reproduce ourselves; emotionally, it means that we must have more of what has made us feel secure in the past. In a chart, the place of the Moon is a place of familiarity that will be resistant to change; in consciousness, the Moon represents the influence of the past that is shaping our desires and values in the present lifetime. These will drive our lives until we consciously review them to see how well they are serving us in the present lifetime.

Mercury

- Natural ruler of the third and sixth houses
- By sign and house position, Mercury indicates where we receive impressions and where and how we seek to express our own perceptions

According to esoteric astrology, Mercury rules the soul. In a chart, it represents the soul. Wherever it appears, it will indicate the area of life in which we will be most attuned to the soul.

Venus

- Natural ruler of second and seventh houses
- By sign and house position, Venus describes who and what attracts us

In popular astrology, Venus is viewed as the prime significator of love. For the esoteric astrologer, Venus rules the process that draws the human personality back towards the soul from the isolation of the state of separation. To whatever or whomever Venus draws us represents a route back from isolation.

Mars

- Natural ruler of the first and eighth houses
- By sign and house position, Mars indicates what we are fired up to pursue

Unlike Venus, which beckons to us from the other side of separation, Mars impels us from the depths of our desire nature, sending us in pursuit of what rouses our passions and generates energy that may be refined and raised to open the heart centre.

In esoteric astrology, Mars represents the emotional body.

Jupiter

- Natural ruler of the ninth and twelfth houses
- By sign and house position, Jupiter indicates those things towards which we feel positive and with which we interact confidently

In a chart, Jupiter indicates the places where we are least inhibited and enjoy feelings of expansiveness. By means of an involvement with the things connected with its placement, we gain experience and understanding.

In esoteric astrology, Jupiter represents the higher planes of the astral body which have a direct connection with the development of the heart chakra.

Saturn

Natural ruler of the tenth and eleventh houses
By sign and house position, Saturn indicates the quality of the mindset that has been forming over lifetimes and which dominates our understanding of life.

Saturn provides the personality with its structure and is responsible for one's basic assumptions about life. Of themselves, assumptions cut us off from new kinds of experiences and different ways of understanding and perceiving. Saturn, therefore, represents familiarity, restriction, limitation, and imbalance. The new direction of the personality represents a challenge to the Saturnian mentality.

Esoterically, Saturn rules the throat centre, the seat of discrimination and decision making.

Uranus

- Natural co-ruler of the eleventh house
- By sign and house placement, Uranus indicates where and how we are to challenge the limitations put in place by the Saturnian mindset

Uranus represents liberation and requires us to relinquish anything that stands to restrict us in the unfolding of our developmental task. The higher octave of Mercury, Uranus serves the soul by destroying the attachments and defences of the personality and setting the intuitive capacity free. Our choice is whether to accept and cooperate with this process, not whether to allow it to go to work in our lives. Over this, we have no control.

Esoterically, Uranus rules the causal, or egoic body, which forms the bridge between the personality and the soul.

Neptune

- Natural co-ruler of the twelfth house
- By sign and house position, Neptune indicates where we seek to diminish our sense of separation and isolation by offering ourselves up to something higher than ourselves

The higher octave of Venus, Neptune appeals to the highest level of personality consciousness and invites it to be aware of what it shares with the soul. Neptune erodes boundaries in order to allow the circumscribed personality to gain a greater sense of belonging to something larger and more significant than self.

Pluto

- Natural co-ruler of the eighth house
- By sign and house position, Pluto indicates a quality of emotional energy which the developing personality is now required to process

Pluto scours the desire nature and discloses attachments and tendencies, which often exist below the threshold of consciousness and which keep the personality in thrall to desire. The higher octave of Mars, Pluto supervises the processing of the energy of desire, which can either be raised to become aspiration or can descend to become physical matter. But nothing in the manifestation can stand still. This unprocessed residue of past lives that Pluto discloses presents a challenge to our present realities, which we will either process and eliminate it or be controlled by it.

Chiron

- Associated with the sixth and ninth houses
- By sign and house position, Chiron indicates situations that have been spiritually challenging to the developing consciousness

Since it entered the planetary pantheon in the 1970s, Chiron has been known as the 'scar upon the Soul'. It indicates a matter that has confused and confounded personality consciousness – one that has not yet been resolved.

Its orbit places Chiron between Saturn and Uranus. As a principle, it occupies the middle ground between holding on and letting go: Chiron demands from the personality a conscious response that is acceptable to the personality and yet acknowledges the perspectives of the soul.

2. Aspects

Aspects are defined as 'the energetic exchange between planets'. Although an understanding of the nature of these exchanges must come from a basic knowledge of astrology, in the present context, there is a purpose for identifying aspects that have a marked effect upon our emotional being and that will condition our experiences in relationship.

The aspects that we will focus on (below) involve the luminaries and significators of the key houses, as identified in the previous lesson. But also to be considered, of course, are the aspects involving planets in key relationship houses.

The Sun

Harmonious aspects to the Sun enable us to find our way to our rightful identity and to a role for ourselves, especially in those areas of life denoted by the houses containing the planets that cast the aspects and those that they rule. When we find a role for ourselves and an outlet for our creativity, we have an opportunity to understand the point of our lives. This draws us towards others with whom we may share this experience of purposefulness and so end the isolation of separation.

Stressful aspects to the Sun indicate that we will have to experience many challenges before we understand and accept our rightful identity. Stressful aspects from the inner planets pull a person in different directions, which works against the formation of an identity. If the Moon is amongst the planets involved in the stressful aspects, then this conflict is likely to be reflected in the differing values and attitudes of the father and mother.

Stressful aspects from the outer planets indicate that we have to go through experiences that will demand us to undergo changes in consciousness before we can see the point of ourselves and make an authentic contribution. The houses containing the challenging planets and those that they rule will be the sources of the conflict, which usually reflect themselves in the relationship, or lack of one, with the father.

The Moon

Harmonious aspects to the Moon indicate a meshing of past and present identities. They enable ease of emotional expression, particularly through the areas of life containing and ruled by the planet or planets involved in the aspect. Harmonious aspects from inner planets to the Moon indicate an affectionate and interactive relationship with the mother, which provides a positive start to relationship life.

Stressful aspects to the Moon indicate that the present lifetime represents a challenge to the old idea of self, which can be a cause of confusion and discomfort. If we honour the memory that makes us feel emotionally safe, we may be aware that we are compromising our potential and our opportunities.

Stressful aspects from inner planets indicate tension in the relationship with the mother, with Saturn denoting a strict and critical mother. Aspects from the outer planets indicate a severing of the bonds between mother and child early in life.

At the level of personality, *stressful* aspects to the Moon, especially from Saturn and the outer planets, are likely to be a cause of very real suffering in life, indicating, as they do, problems with self-image, difficulties in having emotional needs met, and difficulty with receiving from others the kind of feedback that makes us feel at ease with others and with ourselves.

Venus

Harmonious aspects to Venus indicate that we will experience little difficulty in defining and recognising to whom and to what we need to draw close in order to feel whole. Our choices are likely to fit comfortably into the scheme of our lives. Aspects from the outer planets to Venus, which is of great importance to the hierarchy called the human personality, indicate that our choices are assisting more than simply our own development. They are also helping us to move on in consciousness collectively.

Stressful aspects to Venus from the inner planets influence us to make choices that are inconsistent with the tenor of this life overall, pulling us into blind alleys or back into the past. The houses containing the planets and those they rule will show the cause of the distraction.

When Saturn and the outer planets are involved in stressful aspects, then regeneration of the tastes and values is required in order to release us from regressive tendencies. Stressful aspects to Venus from Saturn indicate a cold or rejecting parent, usually the father.

Mars

Harmonious aspects involving Mars and the inner planets increase the energy and enthusiasm available to us. When the outer planets are involved, it indicates that the emotional body and its desires are able to accommodate the developmental requirements of the present lifetime and also provide motivation.

Stressful aspects to Mars have a blocking and frustrating effect: if there are a lot of semi-squares, then the effect is likely to be acute irritability. Squares, conjunctions, and oppositions produce volatility and may attract violence and bullying. If Saturn is involved, then the effect is more subdued but no less denying. It indicates an overbearing parent, usually the father.

When the outer planets are involved in stressful aspects to Mars, this indicates that the desire nature has to be challenged and regenerated to enable it to complement the true identity. With such aspects, there is often a very strong sexual attraction to people with whom we are otherwise incompatible.

Saturn

Saturn's nature is such that there is not a great deal of difference between its effects when working through harmonious or stressful aspects. The *harmonious* aspects to inner planets slow things down and remove spontaneity, whereas the stressful aspects intensify this state of affairs to the point of stymieing the inner planets.

Combining in *stressful* aspect with the Moon, Venus, and Mars, Saturn produces serious emotional and sexual inhibitions. With the Sun and Jupiter, it produces depression. The placement of Saturn and the house that it rules reveal the basic cause of the problem. Lifetimes in which Saturn is a source of obstruction require us to rethink and review the assumptions that are driving our lives before we can release the blocked energy of inner planets.

When the outer planets are involved in *harmonious* aspects with Saturn, it indicates that during the course of the lifetime, the mindset will be subject to the transformative effects of the outer planets working through the areas of life denoted by the houses in which they are to be found. The stressful aspects intensify the process and result in intense and protracted experiences.

Uranus

The planet Uranus supports irrevocable change. The *harmonious* aspects of Uranus, when involving inner planets, produce lightness and adventurousness: we move willingly towards the new and the unusual and easily and beneficially absorb the effects of these things into our consciousness. When the key significators are involved, adventures come into life through the relationships.

When the aspects are *stressful,* change comes in a far more dramatic way, concentrated through specific and often traumatic occurrences. Uranus in stressful aspect to the Moon brings about a severance of the bond with the mother in childhood, the legacy of which is an insecurity that is taken into adult relationships. With Venus, Uranus brings about sudden severances and a tendency towards relationships in which two people cannot live either with or without each other, resulting in innumerable splits and reconciliations. When the relationship is between Venus and Uranus, there will never be stability or consolidation for as long as the object to which we are attracted is redolent of past patterns. With Mars, Uranus can bring physical, emotional, and sexual violence into a life in order to free us from fixations, obsessions, and unproductive attachments.

Pluto

Pluto scours our emotional nature to rid it of the detritus of old patterns. In *harmonious* aspects to the inner planets, Pluto carries out its clean-up operation continuously and gradually, drawing a person towards situations and people that will act as agents in the process. Not infrequently, it will bring the same person into another's life more than once, after an interval of years, if there is unfinished business between them.

In *stressful* aspects, Pluto works in a more intense way, creating difficult and painful situations involving loss and obsession that are designed to make a person aware of his or her own destructive inclinations. Like attracts like on the astral plane. Pluto works through this fact, first to bring awareness, and then liberation from hitherto unacknowledged desires and leanings.

General Considerations: Summary

In applying the information given above to the charts of Hannah and Mark or any natal chart, it should possible to answer the following questions and find out a great deal about the relating self.

1. Direction of the life: What are the implications for relationships (focus upon Sun by sign and house placement)?
2. How many other key significators and key houses are involved with the Sun?
3. Past life legacy: What are the implications for relationships (focus upon Moon and Saturn by sign and house placement)?
4. How many other key significators and key houses are involved with the Moon and Saturn?

5. What is the message of Venus?
6. What is the message of Mars and Pluto?
7. Are any other planets in a position to make them especially influential?

The more we understand about the relating self, the better we will understand the relationships we make.

Endnotes

1. The companion publication to this book, *Working with Time,* focuses on primary and secondary directions and on inner and outer planet transits.
2. We are likely to be more *conscious* of the qualities of our ruling or rising planet, which, of course, is the representative of the Ascendant sign. As we will see in part two, the ruling planet is of importance in synastry.
3. Obviously, the handshake test can be useful in helping to rectify birth time, especially if two signs may be at issue.

Chapter 3

The Relating Self – Esoteric Considerations

1. Esoteric Rulerships

The relating self has an orthodox ruler and an esoteric ruler. Of course, the same is true of those with whom the self relates. Although we will deal with this matter in context of synastry, it is interesting to note what this adds to our understanding of the relating self and to see from what it is derived:

- The ascendant–descendant axis
- The ruling planet

When it comes to the four key relationship houses, to know the esoteric ruler is to know the quality – not just the form – of the experience that is on offer.

- H1 indicates the energy we draw upon to deal with the world. Also, it is a window into the mental body.
- H2 indicates what motivates us to engage with the world. It is also a window into the emotional body.
- H5 indicates our creative capacity and individuality and is another (higher) window into the mental body.
- H7 indicates how we perceive relationship, its function in our lives and the kind of personal relationships that we attract. H7 is a window into the intellectual body.
- H8 indicates the way that others impress our desire nature. It is a window into the emotional body.
- H11 indicates the kind of group that will do justice to our creative contribution. It is another (higher) window into our intellectual body.

Planets in any of these houses will condition our experiences and our understanding in these areas.

We will remind ourselves about the esoteric rulers of each sign in order to prepare ourselves for part two, in which we look at synastry (see endnote 1).

polarity	orthodox rulerships	esoteric rulerships
♈——————♎	♂——————♀	♀——————♅
♉——————♏	♀——————♂	♈——————♂
♊——————♐	☿——————♃	♀——————♁
♋——————♑	☽——————♄	♆——————♄
♌——————♒	☉——————♅	☉——————♃
♍——————♓	☿——————♆	☽——————♇

2. Personality Emphasis and Relationship: The Areas of Consciousness

The term *correspondence* is to be defined as 'the same principle expressing itself on a different level'.

- **Houses 1–4** are the houses of personality consciousness. They correspond to the first aspect of soul, the personality itself.
- **Houses 5–8** are the houses of relating consciousness. They correspond to the second aspect of soul, the egoic aspect.
- **Houses 9–12** are the houses of universal consciousness. They correspond to the third aspect of the soul, or the spiritual soul.

Astrological Houses	**Developmental Task**
Personality consciousness, houses 1–4	Understanding self and personal capacity; producing physical integration and personal effectiveness.
Relating consciousness, houses 5–8	Responding to and understanding others and, through others, producing emotional awareness and balance between self and other.
Universal consciousness, houses 9–12	Purposeful, goal-orientated activity, producing social integration and balance between the individual, the personal relationship, and the group.

It would be a serious oversimplification to deduce that people born with the Sun and inner planets in houses 5–8 are the relationship people of the zodiac. Even so, there is truth in this. The relationships (of all kinds) of people with this emphasis will be of crucial importance to the way they structure their lives.

All of us will have relationships of many kinds during the course of our lifetimes, but the areas of consciousness will decide the focus within the relationship. These will also determine our perception of what we have to give to others, how much we are to give, and how we are to do this. This is a matter of the utmost importance when considering personal relationships, as it is one of the major, albeit unrecognised, reasons for incompatibility. We will return to this in part two.

Following is a list showing the house in which the Sun and inner planets reside along with the attendant focus of a person:

- Personal consciousness; his or her own experience and the learning about self and values that accompanies it. The aim of relationship is to come to know self (personality).
- Relating consciousness; trying to balance his or her needs with those of a partner, the expectations, about whose needs and desires the person will be very aware. The aim of the relationship will be to assist the balancing of self and other (which corresponds to balancing personality and egoic consciousness, or 'alignment').
- Universal consciousness; trying to balance the demands of the relationship with his or her commitment to the cause in which his or her individuality finds its purpose (which corresponds to balancing personality, egoic consciousness, and soul consciousness).

The Lunar Nodes and the Part of Fortune

The Lunar Nodes

The place of the north node identifies the end of the see-saw that remains to be weighed down by experience and consciousness. The place of the south node indicates the quality of consciousness that has been generated by the incarnating process up to this lifetime. The conditioning effect of this upon the approach to relating must be considered.

If the lunar nodes fall into any of the key relationship houses, then this is an indication that consciousness has been developing for lifetimes around the matter of balancing self and other, whether other is another personality or the group.

The planets disposited (see endnote 2) by the node are to be considered together with planets in conjunction and square to the nodal degree. These indicate energies that will be of importance in this task in the present lifetime. If any key significators are involved, then these, too, will have implications for relationship.

The Part of Fortune

For a whole generation of exoteric astrologers, the Part of Fortune was considered to be of great importance in the matter of love.

To the esoteric astrologer, the Part of Fortune is more usefully understood as denoting the nature of the pull from the astral level that has brought us back into incarnation. If it falls in one of the key houses, then the message is clear: there will be a special involvement with this area and any planets that are involved in close aspect with the Part of Fortune, especially through the conjunction or opposition aspect, which will indicate energies that will be of particular importance in determining the nature of these experiences. If it falls in any of the key relationship houses, then the inference of this is obvious, although the esoterically orientated astrologer will have to broaden his or her understanding of the houses to include the *quality* of experiences that each provides.

- In H5, the desire is to know greater individuality and achieve personal recognition.
- In H7, the desire is to know equality and to cooperate.
- In H8, the desire is for emotional involvement (see endnote 3).
- In H11, the desire is to know fellowship and feel purposeful.

This information should be added to any picture being built using the charts of Hannah and Mark, or any natal chart:

- The esoteric rulers
- The areas of consciousness
- Lunar nodes
- Part of Fortune

Endnotes

1. The ideas behind the esoteric considerations offered in this work are examined in this author's book, *Transitional Astrology*.
2. Dispositors are planets which displace the natural ruler of a sign, e.g., Venus in Aries is the dispositor of Mars.
3. This is a very powerful place for the Part of Fortune, as it is comparable to that of a planet in its own sign and in its own house. In H8, the Part of Fortune creates the desire for things that may be destructive to personal relationships, namely power, control, possession, and sensation.

Part Two

Self and Other – Synastry

Chapter 4

Introducing Other

Introduction

The official term for one asking a question of an astrologer is a *quesitor;* the person about whom the question is asked is called the *quesited.* It is useful to have access to these terms when talking synastry.

Synastry is the comparison of the energy fields of two people, undertaken with a view towards gaining insight into the nature of their attraction, antipathy, or indifference to each other, and assessing the way their energy fields will work together.

The prefix *syn* comes from the Greek, meaning 'with' or 'together'.

If the technique is required to analyse the dynamics of more than two people, then each person in the group has to be compared to each of the others. Work on a family unit, for example, requires this kind of treatment. And, yes, this is labour-intensive, but its reward is an awareness that no other discipline can bring.

This branch of astrology uses all the disciplines of orthodox natal astrology:

- Ascertaining the influence of planets in houses, as one partner's planets will fall in the houses of the other.
- Calculating and interpreting aspects, as the planets in one partner's chart will make aspects to certain planets in the other partner's chart. As we will see later in this chapter, *which* planet and *which* aspect determine the quality of the experience that two people have together.
- Progressing charts, as the findings from the progressed charts of two people are a refinement that may be of value in certain situations. The analysis of the natal pattern, however, is by far the most important aspect of synastric work.

Generally speaking, synastric work is flawed by a lack of awareness of the facts of energy distribution. For example, when one person's planet is aspected by the other's slower-moving planet, the individuals will not experience this contact in similar ways. The person with the faster planet will be only too aware of an invasive connection, whilst the person with the slower planet may be oblivious of it. We examine this matter in some detail later in this work.

If clients know about this branch of astrology, they tend to be fascinated by it. It can be very helpful, indeed, in facilitating people's understanding of each other and of the situations they face in their relationships.

But the very fact that synastry involves analysis of another's most personal details, i.e. the birth data, should alert us to an ethical issue. *Is it in order for one person, without the consent of the other, to commission a piece of work that involves the other?* Astrologers must set their own standards for approaching this matter.

Making allowances, of course, for the astrologer's skill in interpreting the evidence, the testimony of a synastric chart is irrefutable. And, it is often unwelcome. So, synastry is not something to be used lightly (see endnote 1). Indeed, it is probable that it never will be used to optimum effect if the quesitor does not have awareness of the many roles that relationships play in the unfolding of consciousness.

We are all involved in the working through of situations set in motion by our own patterns. The experience of incarnating discloses those patterns in the outer world so that we may better observe them and deal with them. A person with awareness will try to understand his or her experiences, especially if an experience in a relationship is a source of disappointment or grief. Few things will test us more than our relationships.

Self and Other: Hannah and Mark

Figure A

Hannah: Synastric comparison with Mark
Geocentric, Tropical, Koch house system
©Winstar Matrix software

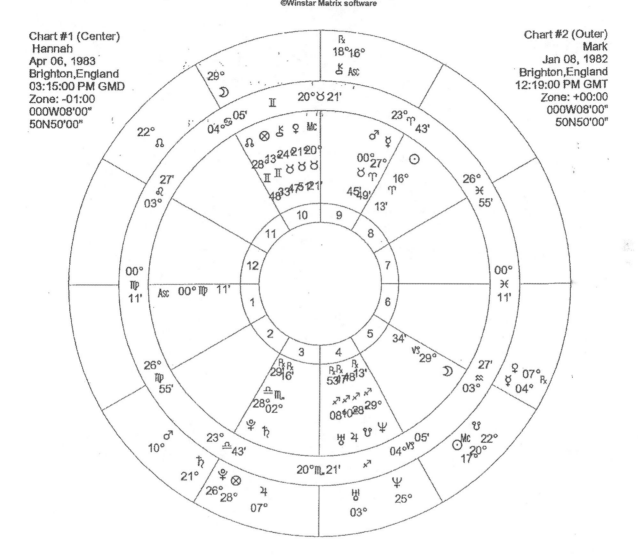

Figure B

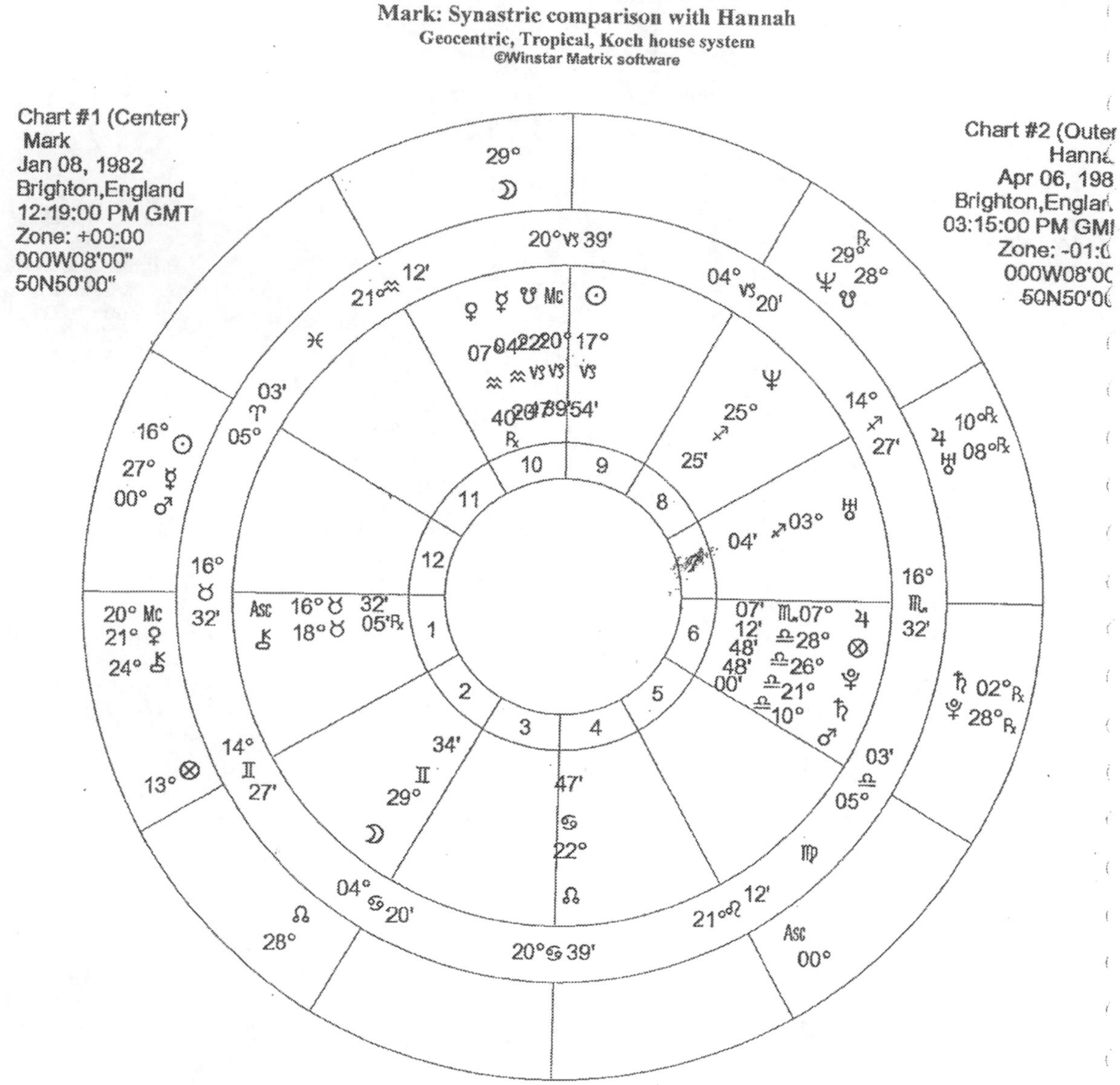

Mark: Synastric comparison with Hannah
Geocentric, Tropical, Koch house system
©Winstar Matrix software

Chart #1 (Center)
Mark
Jan 08, 1982
Brighton,England
12:19:00 PM GMT
Zone: +00:00
000W08'00"
50N50'00"

Chart #2 (Outer
Hanna
Apr 06, 198
Brighton,Englan
03:15:00 PM GM
Zone: -01:0
000W08'00
50N50'00

Hannah

With her Sun in H8, Hannah is learning to be more aware of emotion – in her own life and in others' lives. The presence of the sign Aries indicates that Martian energy will be important in bringing into her life the experiences she needs.

The way forward for Hannah is through emotional involvement with others and loss of self in relationships, leading on, eventually, to a greater awareness of personal truth and discernment in dealings with others – enriched by emotional receptivity.

Inner planets in H9 will assist Hannah in this process of gaining wisdom.

The presence of the Moon in Capricorn's last degree (influence of Aquarius present) on the cusp of H5 and H6 indicates that Hannah has brought through memory of a materialistic and emotionally detached way of dealing with life that has emphasised physical responsibility and hard work.

Saturn in Scorpio in H3 speaks of a deep-rooted pattern of repressed emotionality, poor sexual boundaries within the family, problems with communication, alienation from kin, control of and by kin and community, and restrictions arising in the environment of birth.

The line of least resistance for Hannah is to remain enclosed and restricted by the manipulative family ethic.

The role of relationship in Hannah's life is to bring in some vision and impart a sense of specialness, leading to a greater emotional awareness and a release from restrictions (Neptune in Sagittarius on cusp of H4 and H5 is the significator of relationships), which are the product of a materialistic view of life.

How Hannah is doing so far: With Mark, Hannah surely appears to have found something special, something that has lifted her out of the discontent and unhappiness that she experienced as a child. But she has not got away from the family, especially her mother, with whom she has a very intense and difficult relationship. Hannah's mother is a Capricorn and, in early middle age, is a very attractive but disappointed and resentful woman.

Hannah, in the way of a young eighth-house person, is trying to make up to her mother for her disappointments, even to the extent of giving up her weekends since her mother's second husband left – in order to keep her company. At present, Mark's compliance is making it easy for her to do this, but there is little question that Mark would like to get Hannah away from her mother, whom he considers to be a destructive, discontented person with a self-defeating value system (she wants everything but resents having to work so hard for it). But it is not Mark's way to create waves. The H9 influence is, at present, expressing itself most obviously through Hannah's work in a travel agency. She and Mark do take occasional holidays away because Hannah gets a travel discount, but Hannah feels guilty when they do this. If she takes Mark, then she cannot give her mother the benefits of her discounts. Mark worries about the interruption to his training programme and disappointing his father.

Mark

With his Sun in Capricorn on the cusp of H9 and H10, Mark is learning about material responsibility and leadership.

The way on for Mark is through holding positions of authority and responsibility and gaining control in the matter of steering his own life. This means eventually gaining a greater independence from his father, even though he has been an enormously important role model.

Mark's Moon in the last degree of Gemini (influence of Cancer present) on the cusp of H3 and H4 indicates that the memory is of being much identified with family mores, which include a punitive work ethic. Saturn in Libra in H6 speaks of a deep-rooted assumption of the need to be of service to others, a perspective that encourages a person to be the support act in the lives of others, pushing himself to the limit, physically speaking. The presence of Chiron in H1 indicates that Mark needs to build up his own sense of personal effectiveness.

The line of least resistance for Mark is to remain in a supporting role with family, working hard to please others rather than living in accordance with his own value system.

The role of relationship in Mark's life is to bring him to an awareness of what, in the context of his own evolution, are the more restrictive aspects of relating: over-compliance, over-reliance on family and on getting approval, and to experience a more emotionally rewarding kind of relating. Uranus in H7 speaks of the need for newness to enter his life through his relationships.

How Mark is doing so far: Mark's father was always going to be a dominant figure in his life. At present, Mark's life is cast in the mould of his father. Since he was a child, Mark has been out running with his father. He strives to match his father's achievements in this field. As a consequence, when Mark is not with Hannah, he is training. He works as a fitness instructor in a sports centre. With Capricornian determination and sixth-house preoccupation with the physical vehicle; he frequently pushes his body to the limit. Yet, Mars in Libra is not competitive.

If he dared question it, Mark might find that whilst he enjoys running, he dislikes racing. But, for now, he remains overly identified with the idea of mastery as a physical condition. Like Hannah, he has not yet succeeded in getting free from his family: the paternal value system still stamps his life. Between seeking approval from his father and supporting Hannah, he scarcely has time to consider his own life. Indeed, the idea that he might have a life of his own has not really registered with him in any meaningful way because he is so focused upon keeping people happy and matching up to expectations. One of the things that attracts Mark to Hannah is that she brings feminine energy into a life otherwise dominated by (competitive) masculine values. Hannah is a friend. To be with her, Mark puts up with more than he would choose of Hannah's mother. However, there is no competitiveness within their relationship, which is a relief to him. Hannah, who is very beautiful, is rather weighty, but Mark likes this softness about her. Despite his own concern with his physique, he never suggests to her that she lose weight. With her, Mark can loosen up to some degree. She has brought other values into his life. Hannah sets very little store by Mark's sporting achievements. And she can scarcely be described as impressed by Mark's father, whom she considers vain and image-conscious. She thinks that his efforts to impress women are rather ridiculous and dishonest, especially since she is aware that he does not really like them. She does not see many similarities between her partner and his father, although she resents the latter's influence over Mark.

Endnote

1. Synastry is for established relationships and is not recommended for those who have just met, in which case it is better to allow direct personal experience to alert a person to the desirability of continuing the relationship. In such a situation, being loaded up with prior knowledge is likely to be burdensome rather than helpful.

Chapter 5

The Technique of Synastry 1 – Basic Considerations

The technique of synastry involves the overlaying of two charts in order to see how the planets in the chart of one interact with those of the other, and which areas of life will be most directly influenced by these interactions.

In synastry, we need to be able to distinguish the effects of the Sun, Venus, and Jupiter, which, when charts are overlaid, cooperate with the planets with which they make contact: Mars, Saturn, Uranus, Neptune, and Pluto, which challenge. For the purposes of the synastric exercise, we will call these two groups of planets, respectively, Promoters and Challengers.

The effect of the Moon and Mercury will depend upon whether they make contact with planets within houses. Alone, they are not powerful as relayers of energy into houses.

1. Collecting the Data

I. Legitimacy

Take a view on whether the quesitor has a right to the information requested.

II. Data Tolerance

Obviously, the more accurate the data, the more thorough the job done. This is true across the astrological board, not just with reference to synastry.

In ideal circumstances, the astrologer will have the date, time, and place of birth of both parties. But, because so much in synastry depends upon mutual planetary connections that are not greatly influenced by a matter of hours, it is still possible to do a basic synastric comparison if the time of birth of one partner is unknown. The exception here is the Moon, an important body in any relationship analysis. The orbs of influence take care of this problem to some degree (see endnote 1).

III. Natal Charts

It is advisable to set up the birth charts of both/all individuals involved to see who is involved in this relationship. At a basic minimum, establish the following:

- The life purpose of each partner
- The role of relationship in the life of each (see Part One – The Relating Self)

2. The Overlaying of the Charts

In synastry, analysis is undertaken with the overlaid chart's providing the terms of reference. In effect, the person whose chart is being overlaid becomes the quesited. The inquiry focuses on his or her experience of the relationship. Then, the positions are reversed.

In order to see the situation from both sides, the natal chart of each party should be both overlaid and overlaying.

In Figure A, the overlaid chart is that of Hannah. The synastric comparison with Mark will be undertaken with reference to Hannah.

In Figure B, the situation is reversed. Mark's is the overlaid chart.

This process of overlaying can be done manually or by means of a computer programme. Much astrology software comes with a specific synastry programme. Or, one may adapt a transit programme.

If using software, check to see which aspects are being used and what the allowable orbs of influence are. In Chapter 7, guidance is offered in the matter of the aspects and the maximum orbs recommended for use in synastric work. To work with too many aspects and too-wide orbs is simply cumbersome.

3. The Houses in Synastry

In synastry, as in natal horoscopy, the houses provide the frame, but this structure is meaningful only if the birth times are known. Examining where the planets of the overlaying chart fall on the overlaid chart reveals how and where the quesitor's planetary energies will enter the energy field (reality) of the other. How effectively they do this will depend upon the reception they receive.

If a planet:

- makes contact with a faster planet, either in that house or in another, but makes a harmonious aspect, it will find a way in effortlessly and make a significant impact
- makes no contact with a planet in that house, it will be able to leave an impression upon the area of life that the house represents, in the form of stimulation or repression, depending upon the nature of the planet involved
- makes contact with a slower-moving planet, its entry will be blocked or at least frustrated, depending upon the angle (aspect) of the contact

In terms of relationships, some energies work better through some houses than others. For example, if Uranus in one person's chart is working through H7 of a partner's chart, the effect of this on the relationship life may be disruptive or, at the very least, work against consolidating the relationship – whereas the effect of Venus could be expected to be very different.

This goes some way towards explaining why one person is seen differently by different people. Basically, his or her energy will be received differently by each person.

In general, the following happens:

- When working through the houses of personal consciousness (houses 1–4), the planets which we are designating Promoters (see table following), encourage self-confidence and self-expression; whereas Challengers thwart and provoke. The developmental opportunity for the quesited is to move on to become more aware of self and more self-confident. The gains are personal.
- When working through the houses of relating consciousness (houses 5–8), the Promoters encourage sharing, emotional expression, and cooperation. The Challengers disrupt. The developmental opportunity for the quesited is to move on to become more emotionally aware. The gains include a better understanding of self in relation to other.
- When working through the houses of universal consciousness (houses 9–12), the Promoters encourage involvement in activities and interests outside of the relationship. The Challengers create difficulties for a person in this area. The developmental opportunity for the quesited is to move on to become more connected to others within the larger scheme, however that is understood. The gains are spiritual.

Also to be considered are the houses in which the hylegs fall, because these houses in the life of the quesited will become involved in the expression through those points.

In all cases, the effect of the planet will be either greatly enhanced (if it finds a faster-moving planet in that house with which to interact) or diminished (if a slower-moving planet absorbs it). We will look at this in Chapter 6. But, in any case, the energy of another will only add emphasis to or modify existing patterns. The natal chart shows a person's essence. No external influence has the power to alter that. Whether it is the encouraging effect of a Promoter or the disruptive effect of a Challenger, the effect will still serve the purpose of development.

When considering the effect of one person's planets in the chart of another, always be aware of the areas of life of which those planets are significators, because this will ground the analysis and make it more meaningful.

4. The Influence of the Planets on the Houses

This stage of the process examines how the planets of one party fall on the houses of the other. The charts are then reversed so that each party, in turn, is the quesited.

It is better to tackle synastry in a systematic way, dealing first with one party and then the other, rather than jumping backwards and forwards from one person's reality to the other's. Effective synthesis eludes such an approach.

A. Quesited: Hannah

Area of Consciousness/Hannah	Planet/Hyleg	Quality	Significator in Chart of Mark
Personal/First	-	-	-
Personal/Second	Mars	Promoting	H7 and H12
	Saturn*		
Personal/Third	Saturn	Challenging	H10 and H11
	Pluto	Challenging	H7
	Jupiter	Promoting	H8 and H11
	Descendant		
Personal/Fourth	Uranus	Challenging	H11
	Neptune	Challenging	H11
Relating/Fifth	Sun	Promoting	H5
	MC		
Relating/Sixth	Mercury	Absorbing	H2 and H5
	Venus R.	Promoting	Ascendant and H5
Relating/Seventh	-	-	-
Relating/Eighth	-	-	-
Universal/Ninth	Ascendant		
Universal/Tenth	Moon*	Absorbing	H3
Universal/Eleventh	Moon	Absorbing	H4

Universal/Twelfth	-	-	-

* Technically in this house, but because it is within 5 degrees of the house cusp, its influence falls in the next.

Commentary

In Hannah's chart, the area of 'Personal Consciousness' receives the most input from Mark's planets. With the exception of Jupiter, all of the planets are challenging, indicating that in Hannah's life, Mark has been an agent for change, specifically in matters pertaining to H3 and H4, which show the early environment, education, and home. Hannah met Mark when she was very young. Since the age of fourteen, her life has been centred upon him, taking her away from her own family and exacerbating an already difficult relationship with her mother, who is becoming increasingly disenchanted with men. Hannah's mother is almost compelled to think that her daughter is making herself unhealthily reliant upon Mark. Hannah thinks that her mother has just not met the right man and is becoming bitter.

It is also possible that had Hannah not met Mark, she would have gone off to college like her girlfriends. Hannah's mother would have liked this for her daughter because it was an opportunity that she herself did not have. Hannah's mother believes that her lack of education is the reason why she has to work so hard now in a job that is uncongenial to her (she is an assistant in a fashion shop). Saturn, which is the significator of Mark's H9, H10, and H11, suggests that in Mark's family, college is not part of the culture. His father is a practical, hardworking, self-employed man (working in the field of IT) and a serious sportsman. Mark is both influenced and motivated by him. But in Mark's natal chart, Venus in H10 is retrograde, which indicates that Mark will have a change of heart about authority figures and their goals.

On account of their sense of commitment to their respective parents, neither Mark nor Hannah has yet moved more than a couple of miles away from home.

H5 and H11 suggest that Mark has opened up Hannah emotionally, has made her better able to communicate about her emotions, and has made her more sociable.

This is certainly borne out by the change. Hannah transformed from a sullen child to a talkative young adult. Hannah appears to be never not talking to Mark, although there is no evidence of her greater sociability, as they spend most of their time together, mostly alone. Hannah does, however, attend Mark's running club fixtures and mixes quite confidently with his colleagues.

In the houses of the relating area of consciousness, only H5, the House of Creativity, receives input from the Sun. This indicates a strong physical attraction, which has had the effect of awakening Hannah to her own sexuality and creative potential, although the couple have yet to have children, something to which Mark says he is opposed. Mark's Midheaven (MC) falls here, too, which indicates that Hannah's creativity is a determinant of his own expectations and goals.

In the houses of universal consciousness, only the Moon, which relays no great influence, is to be found. It will be noted, however, that Mark's Moon falls on Hannah's north node. The effect of this will be considered in Chapter 6.

Mark's Ascendant falls in Hannah's H9, but it is so close to the cusp as to make its influence felt in H10. This binds together in a most significant way Mark's personality and Hannah's goals and expectations.

From the age of fourteen, Hannah's life has been shaped by her relationship with Mark. She has made crucial decisions with the desire to maintain the relationship at the top of her list of priorities.

It is to be noted that Hannah's Sun is in H8. The challenges to her family life and educational prospects introduced by Mark's presence in her life may not be at all comfortable, but she accepts them as the price she has to pay to be with him. An H8 person will make enormous sacrifices for intimacy.

B. Quesited: Mark

Area of Consciousness/House	Planet/Hyleg	Quality	Significator in Chart of Hannah
Personal/First	Venus	Promoting	H3 & 10
	M.C.		
Personal/Second	North Node		
Personal/Third	-		H11
Personal/Fourth	-		
Relating/Fifth	Ascendant		
Relating/Sixth	Saturn	Challenging	H5 & 6
	Pluto	Challenging	H4
Relating/Seventh	Jupiter R.	Promoting	H4, 7 & 8
	Uranus R.	Challenging	H6
Relating/Eighth	Neptune R.	Challenging	H7 & 8
Universal/Ninth	-		
Universal/Tenth	Moon	Absorbing	H11

Universal/Eleventh	-		
Universal/Twelfth	Mercury	Absorbing	H1, 2, 10
	Sun	Promoting	H12
	Mars	Promoting	H12

Commentary

From overlaying Mark's chart with that of Hannah, it can be seen that it is the area of relating consciousness that receives the most stimulation from Hannah's planets. It will be noted that the planets involved with this area of Mark's chart are, in the main, significators of Hannah's own houses of relating consciousness. Hannah's Jupiter, which is the significator of her H7 and H8, is particularly important here. But so, too, is Uranus, the planet about which, in the context of synastry, there is much to say and which we will be considering in the next lesson.

With regard to steering the relationship through emotional situations, Hannah is the more confident. Mark takes his cue from her and tends to fall in with her suggestions. He is supportive rather than initiating, captivated by her feminine view on things. He does not appear to rate his own male instincts very highly. His attitude is 'Hannah knows best' when it comes to emotional matters, although in all other areas, Hannah expects Mark to come up with the solutions. He accepts this responsibility. She considers that he is the ingenious one and that she is the support act. It should be noted, however, that Mark holds very negative views about marriage. At present, he does not want children. He does not view this as the way forward for him and Hannah. On this matter, he is uncharacteristically vehement. Just out of her teens, Hannah is ambivalent about this and, at present, is saying that she does not mind.

As Hannah's MC falls in Mark's H1 and her Ascendant in his H5, Mark is part of Hannah's moving on in her physical lifestyle.

The presence of three of Hannah's planets in Mark's H12 indicates that, through her, Mark has developmental opportunity to lay the past to rest. She is part of his moving on to a more subtle level and in a more indirect way.

In terms of spiritual development, however, both contributions are equally valid.

Neither Mark not Hannah thinks in such terms. They both appreciate what they have in each other and consider themselves lucky to have met, but there is no awareness of or interest in a larger plan.

Summary

The energy structure behind the strong relationship of these two is now discernible in outline.

Hannah is enabling Mark (Moon in Gemini/H3) to develop a greater awareness of the emotional content and quality of relationship. He has the potential to help Hannah (Moon in Capricorn/H6) to move away from the restricting preoccupation with materialism and security by challenging her upbringing. Their support for each other enables them to deal with the fears arising from their breaking into new ways of being.

How well they are able to perform these roles depends upon the detail in the form of the planetary connections, at which we will look next.

Endnote

1. If neither party knows the exact time of birth, then the problem involving the Moon's placement is more significant. Also, there will be other deficiencies, namely no hylegs to set the house cusp and therefore no individual birth charts at which to look first. Think twice about undertaking proper synastric work in these circumstances, but agree, perhaps, to look at specific problems in light of what can be picked up at the planetary level.

Chapter 6

The Technique of Synastry 2 – The Planets in Synastry

Introduction

In synastry, the mutual contact between the natal planets in the charts of two people provide the dynamic of the association and condition its unfolding. This is the crucial detail that makes or breaks relationships.

In synastry, because our relationships belong to our personality life, it is customary to use the orthodox rather than the esoteric rulerships. The exceptions to this custom are the esoteric rulers of the Ascendant–Descendant. In the case of advanced people, Vulcan and the esoteric rulers of the MC–IC (cusp of H4)axis may also be considered.

Progressed Planets

For the purposes of a synastric exercise, the contacts of prime importance are those between the natal planets. The contact made by progressing planets is influential and may be instrumental in bringing two people together in time and space. But contact made by progression does not alter the basic structure of the relationship any more than the progression of the planets alters the design of an individual life, which is captured in the natal chart. Esoterically, however, it is said *that it is all there in the beginning,* and the planetary aspects in force at the time of the (physical) meeting will shed their light over the participants' *experience* of the relationship.

In the case of a mother and child, that first meeting is considered to be the moment of birth – and that first moment is captured in the child's natal chart. For most other meetings, this is not the case. So, looking at the planetary energies in force at the level of progression and transit at the time of meeting is a useful but supplementary exercise, in essence. The basic synastric exercise requires the two natal charts.

Asteroids and Midpoints

As in all areas of astrology, the picture can be made more detailed by the addition of asteroids and a focus upon midpoints. These should be viewed as possible areas for research and experimentation (see endnote 1).

There is only one midpoint upon which we are going to focus in this course, and that is the midpoint between the Sun and the Moon, known to an earlier generation of astrologers as the Point of Equidistance. It is a point of significance in the matter of synthesising past and present.

As the basic developmental requirement of any lifetime is to 'get off the Moon and behind the Sun', a planet in one person's chart that falls on the Point of Equidistance in another's chart will have bearing upon this undertaking. The nature of the planet, its natural affinity to either the Sun or the Moon, and a person's own relationship with this planetary energy – something that has to be assessed from the natal chart – will determine whether contact to this point will help or hinder this endeavour.

A method for calculating the Point of Equidistance is given at the end of this lesson.

In synastry, the nodes and the hylegs are important points. Planetary contact to these points should be noted. Also of importance is the Part of Fortune. Planetary contact to these points should also be noted.

In all the above cases, the contacts of significance are those made through the conjunction and opposition aspect.

1. Planetary Distribution

Disciplines in respect of planetary motion have their place in this exercise: the slower-moving planet will always influence the faster-moving planet. This holds true between charts, i.e. in synastry as it is within a chart. *This means that in order to distribute its energy to maximum effect, every planet relies upon taking over a faster-moving planet.*

The distribution arrangements between planets are a matter of considerable importance in synastry. It is not given enough importance in books on the subject. The result is that it is usually not specified which party is the beneficiary of a planetary contact.

The tables below are based on the relative motion of the planets and the law that the slower planet influences the faster. To put it another way, the faster planet is passive in relation to the slower and can be commandeered for the purposes of distribution.

	Moon	Mercury	Venus	Sun	Mars	Jupiter	Saturn	Chiron	Uranus	Neptune	Pluto
Moon distributes through:											
Mercury distributes through:	•										
Venus distributes through:	•	•									
Mars distributes through:	•	•	•								
Sun distributes through:	•	•	•								
Mars distributes through:	•	•	•	•							
Jupiter distributes through:	•	•	•	•	•						
Saturn distributes through:	•	•	•	•	•	•					
Chiron distributes through:	•	•	•	•	•	•	•				
Uranus distributes through:	•	•	•	•	•	•	•				
Neptune distributes through:	•	•	•	•	•	•	•	•	•		
Pluto distributes through:	•	•	•	•	•	•	•	•	•	•	

When the planets are in the overlaying chart, they are distributors trying to find a way into the other party's energy field, as shown through the chart of that person. As described in Chapter 2, unless they are able to make contact with planets in the chart of another, the Moon and Mercury will not impress themselves on the other in any noticeable way. The other planets are able to distribute their energy into the houses in the ways described there, although all distribution is greatly enhanced by planetary contact.

When the planets are in the overlaid (quesited's) chart, they are recipients and are either welcoming or repelling the distributed energy, depending upon their natures and capacity to receive.

	Mercury	Venus	Sun	Mars	Jupiter	Saturn	Chiron	Uranus	Neptune	Pluto
Moon receives from:	•	•	•	•	•	•	•	•	•	•
Mercury receives from:		•	•	•	•	•	•	•	•	•
Venus receives from:			•	•	•	•	•	•	•	•
Sun receives from:				•	•	•	•	•	•	•
Mars receives from:					•	•	•	•	•	•
Jupiter receives from:						•	•	•	•	•
Saturn receives from:							•	•	•	•
Chiron receives from:								•	•	•
Uranus receives from:									•	•
Neptune receives from:										•

What we have to consider in synastry is the impact of a planet in one chart – for example, Venus meeting with the same planet in another. Obviously, this situation is unknown in natal astrology. The effect is that of convergence: if the aspect is harmonious, the two planets will flow together; if it is stressful, they will clash. Because they are both different expressions of the aspects of the same energy, one will not prevail over the other in terms of planetary strength, but the difference in mode (determined by sign) will be a source of difference in the relationship. Venus in Leo and Venus in Pisces cannot fail to misunderstand and thwart each other.

Planetary Natures

The Absorbers: The Moon and Mercury

Planet	As a distributor i.e., in the overlaying chart	As a recipient i.e., in the chart of the quesited
Moon • The old idea of self which responds to what is familiar. • The physical body	The Moon cannot distribute because there is no faster moving celestial body. When it does make contact with planets, it absorbs the energy of the planet involved and *reflects back an emotional response in accordance with the nature of the contacting planet to the person with the overlaying chart.* *In the case of making contact with key points, the Moon reflects back a sense of involvement with the out working of matters connected with those points.*	The Moon absorbs the energy of all other planets. As the Moon denotes a past idea of self, contacting planets will either support or challenge this idea. The impact of this upon a person's experience in a relationship is marked. Challenging contacts to the Moon create emotional discomfort in the person whose Moon is thus influenced because they thwart that person's expectation which does not bode well for relationships in which consolidation is expected.
Mercury • The principle of communication	Mercury can distribute its influence into another's energy field only through the Moon and when it does this it creates a strong sense of familiarity, especially when the contact is through the conjunction aspect. The harmonious aspects assist communication between two people and the stressful aspects indicate different modes of communication which give rise to misunderstandings and hurt feelings in the case of the Moon person.	Mercury absorbs influences from all planets except the Moon. This means that it takes into the area of life (house) in which it falls the energy of the planets with which it makes contact, *and brings that energy directly into consciousness of the quesited.* Like the Moon, Mercury, although not a powerful distributor, is planet of great significance as a recipient and when blended with the Promoters it has something positive to communicate; with the Challengers its message is upsetting to the reality of the quesited.

The Promoters

Planet	As a distributor i.e., in the overlaying chart	As a recipient i.e., in the chart of the quesited
Venus • The principle of attraction	The energy of Venus is distributed by the Moon, Mercury, and the key points which is why contact to these points are of such significance in synastry. Without it, the energy of Venus is not able to make much impact upon the other party.	Venus is a recipient of the energy of the two other Promoters (Sun & Jupiter) and all the Challengers. These contacts affect the way a person feels about his experience of giving out to the other. The Promoters make him / her feel good about sharing; the Challengers make it a difficult, joyless experience.
Sun • The present identity	The Sun takes vitality into the area of life (house) in which it falls, where its effectiveness will be dependent upon its reception. If it is drawn in by the Moon, Mercury, Venus or the key points it can be supportive; if it meets with the Challengers then its effect will be diminished.	With the exception of Jupiter, the Sun is a recipient only of the energies of all the challenging planets and when they make contact they greatly influence a person's sense of self and assessment of his or her own ability to cope with life.
Jupiter • The principle of expansiveness	Jupiter offers its expansiveness to the area of life (house) in which it falls. It can be blocked by the Challengers (except Mars) but it will be welcomed in by the inner planets which will bring confidence, comfort and opportunity. Through	Jupiter receives only from the Challengers, and Saturn has the power and inclination to crush it. With the outer planets, however, Jupiter is able to cooperate and steps down their transformative power and makes it easier for the personality to handle.

The Challengers

With regard to the challengers, the aspect involved in the contact is very important and will make the difference between a contact's producing creative tension (harmonious aspects) and making a flow in certain areas of life impossible (stressful aspects). We will be looking at aspects more closely in Chapter 7.

Planet	As a distributor i.e., in the overlaying chart	As a recipient i.e., in the chart of the quesited
Mars • The principle of assertion • Ruler of the Emotional body	The energy of Mars distributes itself using the inner planets, and its effect on them is provocative. With the Absorbers its effect is overbearing and in a relationship when this contact is present it can be very wearing for the person whose Moon / Mercury is involved, although the degree of the discomfort will be determined by the nature of the aspect. The harmonious aspects will lessen the discomfort considerably. Aspects from Mars to the inner planets especially the Moon and Venus promote sexual attraction.	Only Saturn can overwhelm Mars and the effect of this can be deeply distressing in relationships, depending upon the aspects involved. Almost always it saps the initiative and affects the sex life and creates bitterness and resentment in the person whose Mars is suppressed. With Neptune, Mars loses it fieriness and becomes submissive. With the other Challengers Mars retains its volatile nature and can become explosive when the contact is through a stressful aspect and this nearly always threatens the longevity of a relationship.
Saturn • The principle of restriction • Ruler of the Mental body	In synastry, Saturn's influence is all important because, of its nature, it binds. When it interacts with the Promoters it subdues them and makes the person whose inner planets are so overshadowed feel heavy, joyless and lacking in confidence. Yet that connection, uncomfortable though it may be, is likely to create a connection of	Saturn is obliged to receive energy from Chiron, Uranus, Neptune and Pluto, all of which challenge its dominant place in the reality of the personality. But Saturn does not blend with these planets. It tries, rather, to resist them, because that is its nature. Dependent upon the aspect, the outer planets will either chivvy or topple Saturn, arousing great fear in the

	considerable durability and bind two people together for, from the point of view of the personality, better or worse. This state of affairs is influenced to some degree by the nature of the contact that it makes with a planet, but regardless of the aspect Saturn's touch is both heavy and holding.	person whose Saturn is being challenged in this way. When the contact from the outer planets is through stressful aspects, the relationship is put under serious strain.
Chiron • The principal of spiritual challenge • The 'scar on the soul'	Chiron brings creative tension into the area of life into which it falls, especially when it meets there with faster moving planets. It blends with the energy of both Promoters and Challengers alike to produce consciousness awakening situations.	Uranus, Neptune and Pluto all have the ability to commandeer Chiron for their own purposes. When this happens, Chiron blends their energy into the Chironic problem.
Uranus • The principal of Liberation • Agent of the Soul	Uranus the liberator works with a light touch with the promoters and in an incandescent way with the Challengers. When the Promoters welcome it in through making contact, Uranus brings in inspiration, excitement and newness, although rarely stability, into the life of the person whose chart is being overlaid. When he imposes himself upon the Challengers he brings disruption which makes it very difficult for a relationship to consolidate no matter how one or both parties in a relationship might want this at the level of the personality.	Uranus receives energy from both Neptune and Pluto, allowing Neptune to add a mystical, abstruse quality to the work of liberation that it is surely doing. With Pluto, its work of emancipation is more intense and emotionally polarised but, in both cases, the interchange takes place outside the range of consciousness and is rarely recognised as coming from the other party and as such they work behind the scenes in the relationship.

Neptune • The principal of transfiguration	When Neptune is welcomed in by the Promoters it can produce a sublime state in the quesited that fires him or her with enthusiasm for the relationship and when it meets with the Challengers, Neptune takes away their sting. When the contact is made through a stressful aspect then delusion will be a feature of the relationship.	When Neptune receives energy from Pluto it adds transformative energy to Neptune's transfigurative capacity. But, as noted above, in connection with Uranus, the interchange takes place outside the range of consciousness and is rarely recognised as coming from the other party.
Pluto • The principal of transformation	Pluto adds depth and intensity to any planet that it contacts, Promoter or Challenger, and makes the encounter transformative.	

Calculating the Point of Equidistance

The Point of Equidistance is always the midpoint of the *shortest* distance between the Sun and the Moon. It should *always* be calculated by moving in the direction of the signs.

Give the following values to each sign:

Aries: 0

Taurus: 1

Gemini: 2

Cancer: 3

Leo: 4

Virgo: 5

Libra: 6

Scorpio: 7

Sagittarius: 8

Capricorn: 9

Aquarius: 10 Pisces: 11

Thus, Hannah's Sun at Aries 16 degrees, 13 minutes becomes 0 16 13. The Moon at Capricorn 29 degrees, 34 minutes becomes 9 29 34.

Deduct placement of Moon from placement of Sun to find the *shortest* distance between them:

[1]00 16 13
09 29 34 –
02 16 39

[1] Add 12 (00 + 12 = 12) to make sum workable.

Divide this result by 2 = 1 08 19.

Add this to placement of Moon.

09 29 34
01 08 19 +
11 [2]07 53

[2] Carry 30 because there are only 30 degrees in a sign.

Therefore, the Point of Equidistance is <u>Pisces 7 degrees, 53 minutes.</u>

Mark's Sun at Capricorn 17 degrees, 54 minutes becomes 09 17 54.

His Moon at Gemini 29 degrees, 34 minutes becomes 03 29 34.

Deduct placement of Sun from Moon to find *shortest* distance between them.

[3]3 29 34
 9 17 54 –
 6 11 40

[3] Add 1 2 (3+12=15) to make sum workable.

Divide this result by 2 = 3 05 50

Add to placement of Sun.

09 17 54
03 05 50 +
[4]12 23 44

[4] Deduct 12 = 0.

Therefore, Mark's Point of Equidistance is <u>Aries 23 degrees, 44 minutes.</u>

Endnote

1. In the practice of astrology, less is often more. There are merits in intentionally keeping to a minimum the amount of information that has to be synthesized, if it is to be offered back in any coherent way. But, clearly, this is a matter of personal style. Students must find their own level. Some astrologers, working from the assumption that relationships are about balance, lean very heavily upon midpoints in their synastric work.

Chapter 7

The Technique of Synastry 3 –
The Aspects and the Orbs of Influence

Introduction

In all cases, the degree of the impact of the slower-moving planet upon the faster-moving planet is determined by the angle (aspect) from which contact is made, but the quality of the energy exchange is basically the same, regardless of the aspect. *The stressful aspects use this energy to challenge the reality of the other party, whilst the harmonious aspects use it to promote and encourage the other party's personality expression.*

Synastric aspects are to be savoured because of the story they tell! Lay them out in a way that assists you in discovering the story. If using computer software, depending upon the programme, aspects to Chiron, the Point of Equidistance, the nodes, and the Part of Fortune may have to be ascertained separately by examining the charts.

In synastry, the calculation of aspects conforms in every respect to the way in which aspects are calculated for a natal chart, e.g.:

- A planet at 9 degrees Gemini in one chart is in trine aspect to a planet at 6 degrees Libra in the chart of the other party, with an orb of influence of 3 degrees.

In synastry, however, the orbs of influence tend to be tighter, and the range of aspects used is *usually* restricted to the most common major and minor aspects:

conjunction
semi-sextile
semi-square
sextile
trine
quincunx
sesqui-quadrate
opposition

But, as with midpoints, some astrologers who specialize in synastry use aspects that they believe are particularly significant across charts (see endnote 1).

Unsurprisingly, there is no universally accepted agreement on the orbs of influence, but the following may be used as a guide:

- 2 degrees for a minor aspect involving two planets; 3 degrees for a planet and a key point
- 3 degrees for a minor aspect involving a planet and a luminary; 5 degrees for a luminary and a key point
- 5 degrees for major aspects involving two planets
- 5 degrees for a minor aspect between two luminaries
- 7 degrees for a major aspect between a planet and a luminary
- 10 degrees for a major aspect between two luminaries

Where the key points are concerned, only the conjunction and the opposition need be considered.

It is customary to present the aspects in a grid. All software appears to use this format. To the student, however, this presentation may be confusing because it does not make apparent who is the recipient of this contact. In applying the technique, it is therefore recommended to take information from such a grid and lay it out differently, as shown below.

1. The Nature of the Aspects

- The conjunction and the opposition are the most intense and dominant.
- The square is the most antagonizing.
- The semi-square is provocative.
- The injunct (quincunx) and sesqui-quadrate are sources of overreaction.
- The semi-sextile, the sextile, and the trine are supportive.

The Conjunction

Of all aspects used in synastry, the conjunction is the most powerful connection across charts. In the conjunction, the slower planet takes over the faster and finds an effective point of entry into the energy field of the other party.

Some conjunctions are hostile takeovers. Others are friendly. In either case, the impact on the relationship will be marked. The person who has the slower-moving planet will dominate in the area of life indicated by the house in which the conjunction falls. This may indicate dominance in the relationship as a whole, but that would depend upon other factors, notably, the importance of that energy principle – not simply in the relationship, but also in the life of the person experiencing the domination as well as in the life of the person who is dominating. This is why it is so important to study the individuals before looking at the relationship dynamic.

Table of Conjunctions

	☉	☽	☿	♀	♂	♃	♄	⚷	♅	♆	♇	All key points
☉	B	H	N	H	C	H	C	C	C	H	C	H
☽		B	N	H	C	H	C	C	C	H	C	H
☿			B	H	C	H	C	C	C	C	C	N
♀				B	C	H	C	C	C	H	C	H
♂					B	H	C	C	C	C	C	C
♃						B	C	C	H	H	C	H
♄							B	C	C	C	C	C
⚷								B	N	C	C	C
♅									B	B	C	C
♆											B	C

Key:
H = harmonious
C = challenging
N = neutral
B = blending

The Stressful Aspects – Challenging Realities

The Opposition

In synastry, the opposition adds the element of detachment to the learning situation. If the conjunction indicates domination and control, then the opposition introduces distance. In a relationship, the opposition aspect frequently means that the person with the faster-moving planet is separated from the person with the slower-moving planet. This may not be at all because either party consciously wants this but because of the situation in which both find themselves. The separation is the means of awareness to the person with the faster-moving planet, especially if it is an inner planet. The opposition may also express itself through emotional remoteness or resistance, as in the case of the person with the slower-moving planet backing off from the other.

The Square

The square produces arguments and disagreements in long-term relationships in a way that the conjunction and opposition, which give clear supremacy to the slower-moving planet, do not. Ninety degrees is not such an easy angle from which to apply consistent pressure. Periodically, the faster-moving planet can and will find the opportunity to retaliate. Hence the arguments and disputes.

The person with the slower-moving planet will be, however, the most inflexible and better able to thwart the energy expression of the faster-moving planet.

In relationships in which two people may not have to come into contact with each other all that much, the square will be experienced as a no-go area (see endnote 2).

The Semi-Square

This is only a minor aspect. Just as it produces irritability in a natal chart, so it introduces friction into a relationship.

The Injunct

With the injunct, the two planets making contact are out of step with each other and are unable to pull together. The result is tension and stress. Poor timing is frequently a feature of this aspect. If inner planets are involved, then this is more evident and manifests as two people's inability to be in the same frame of mind at the same time. The person with the faster-moving planet is more aware of the strain.

The Sesqui-Quadrate

The sesqui-quadrate is the aspect of overreaction which creates misunderstanding, unhelpful emotionality, and drama between two people. It is especially evident when the inner planets are involved. Although only a minor aspect, more than one sesqui-quadrate in the synastry puts a relationship under considerable strain. The person with the faster-moving planet is more aware of the tension.

The Harmonious Aspects – Supporting and Encouraging Personality Expression

The Trine

When the trine aspect is a feature of the synastry, the slower-moving planet assists the development in the other party's life of the energy principle represented by the faster-moving planet. It is, therefore, a very constructive aspect (see endnote 3). Perhaps all relationships need a couple of trines if they are to stay the course.

The Sextile

The sextile is supportive. Unlike its role in the trine, the slowing-moving planet is not involved so much in developing the faster-moving planet. Instead, it offers approval, cooperation, and acceptance. Relationships in which sextiles dominate the synastry tend to be smooth and supportive.

The Semi-Sextile

Although only a minor aspect, the semi-sextile derives its value from the fact that a small amount of support is better than no support at all.

Collecting the Evidence

In part one, we described the relationship between Hannah and Mark as, according to all appearances, one characterized by compatibility, harmony, and friendship. In this section, we do a synastric exercise to look at the relationship from the inside.

We will look at the situation first from Hannah's point of view, identifying the planets/key points in her chart which are aspected by Mark's slower-moving planets *and which let his energy into her energy field.*

Hannah:

☽∧☽	☉□☉	☿☌♄	♀△☉	♂☍♃	♃∠♇	♄\♅	⚷∧♄	♆☌♆
☽☌☿	☉☍♂	☿△♆	♀∧♄	♂☍♀		♄✶♆	⚷∧♆	♆✶♀
☽✶♅	☉☍♄	☿☍♇				♄☌♇	⚷∧♇	
☽□♇	☉△⚷							
	☉⚼♅							
	☉△♆							

M△☉	A□♅	☊☌☽
M∧♄	A△♆	☋☌♆
	A✶♇	⊗☍♃

- Total number of conjunctions with Mark's planets: 4
  - Harmonious: 3
  - Stressful: 1
- Total number of harmonious aspects received from Mark's planets: 9
- Total number of stressful aspects received from Mark's planets: 13

Closest aspects (not more than 1 degree orb):

♀∧♄

☽∧☽

☉□☉

☉△⚷

☊☌☽

This task requires a lot of concentration! It is easy to lose the plot. But once it is laid out in this way, it is easier to get at the information required, *i.e. to get information about the way Mark interacts with Hannah's value system:*

- Identify the significator of values (in this case, Mercury, which, in Hannah's chart, rules H2, the House of Values and Possessions).
- Examine the contact that Mark's planets make to it.
- Note any planets from Mark's chart working through this house in Hannah's chart.

We will use this approach now to assess how constructive the relationship is in helping Hannah move off the Moon and get behind her Sun, which is the basic developmental requirement of all of us in incarnation.

To do this, we will review aspects to Hannah's:

- Moon
- Sun
- Saturn
- Key points

1. An examination of aspects to the Moon reveals:

   - A useful blend of promoting and challenging aspects. The fact that the respective Moons of Hannah and Mark are in close and tense aspect (injunct with an orb of less than 1 degree) indicates that they have different assumptions about life. This may not be comfortable, but it is useful in creating its own kind of challenge to conditioned behaviour and assumptions.
   - A far more powerful challenge issues from Mark's Pluto (square aspect with an orb of influence of less than 3 degrees). Challenge aspects from Pluto to the Moon are hard to handle in the context of close relationships because the Moon person's feelings and self-image are hurt by the rough energy of the other's Pluto. On the surface, this is rather surprising to find in the chart of these two people who seem so harmonious. But the fact is that Hannah (H8 Sun) has Moon square a conjunction of Saturn and Pluto in her natal chart. She is accustomed to people close to her being hurtful, which, of course, is not without its own significance. The situation between Mark and Hannah is greatly assisted by the contact between her Moon and his Mercury, which is a soft contact that assists communication and creates a sense of harmony. Even so, that square from Pluto should not be overlooked. Pluto is the co-ruler of Mark's seventh house. Almost certainly, he uses this energy unconsciously, and so, unconsciously, he is issuing a major challenge to the assumptions that Hannah has about herself and about her life, including commitment. Mark is very resistant to the idea of marriage, in part because of his experiences of his parents' acrimonious divorce. This is likely to become a big issue between Mark and Hannah. But, for now, the sextile from Mark's Uranus to Hannah's Moon will help her to be accepting of the challenges he creates because she likes the newness he is bringing into her life. But deep down, Hannah will feel rejected by Mark's resistance to the idea of marriage.

2. An examination of the aspects to the Sun reveals:

   - A much stronger pattern of challenge. With reference to the Sun, the challenging aspects must be viewed as a potential obstacle to development, especially when the partner's Saturn is involved. The respective Suns of these two people are square, indicating incompatible life directions. Falling close to the cusp of Hannah's H3 is the opposition from Mark's Saturn, which is not only to her Sun but also to her Mercury in H9. This will make it difficult for her to move on, whether geographically or in terms of new ideas. Because of her relationship with Mark (or so Hannah's mother claims), Hannah did not go on to college. Because of Mark's training programme, running fixtures, and work ethic, the couple do not go away on holiday as often as they could. These are specific and relatively small examples, but there is a larger issue here: Mark's Saturn problem stands to impact Hannah in a very direct way. If she allows it, it will restrict her as it restricts him. The fact that the opposition aspect is involved may indicate that, eventually, this will drive them apart.

3. An examination of Hannah's Saturn reveals:

    - A blend of cooperation from Mark's Uranus and Neptune and a major challenge from Pluto. Again, this may not be comfortable, but it has great transformative power.

4. An examination of the key points reveals:

    - The conjunction of the north node and Mark's Moon will make Mark seem very familiar to Hannah. It gives him a role in her ongoing development. The conjunction made by his Neptune to her south node on the cusp of H5 stands to be a big distraction by 'beguiling' her with what, for the purposes of her development, she needs to leave behind: an immersion in her family of origin. She may not like Mark's father, but Mark's loyalty to him is comfortingly familiar.
    - Although Mark's Sun trines Hannah's MC, indicating compatible goals, his Saturn makes a tense and non-constructive aspect to it, which will have a frustrating effect upon her efforts to move forward.
    - Whilst the Ascendant–Descendant axis receives cooperation from Neptune and Pluto, Mark's Uranus – which, natally, is in H7 – is in square aspect. This introduces an instability factor that we will look at more closely through the frame of Mark's chart. Albeit unconsciously, Mark will be resistant to the idea of formalizing his relationship with Hannah, valuing it for now rather than for what it may be in the future. In time, this is likely to become a source of difficulty for Hannah, who has Venus in Taurus and who is likely to want the stability of formal commitment.

Summary

The conclusion to be drawn here on this matter of whether her relationship with Mark is helping Hannah move on has to be that his very presence in her life is challenging her very basic assumptions that keep her in a habitual way of being. To that extent, it is an important relationship. But what Mark is opening up for Hannah by helping her challenge her own upbringing, he is also shutting down by subjecting her to another set of restrictions based upon his own Saturn problem, which, amongst other things, is making him, at least for now, live out his father's life. One of the closest aspects in their synastry is an exact injunct from Mark's Saturn to Hannah's Venus. Hannah is aware of this to some degree, but she is inclined to blame Mark's father's 'influence' rather than to see it as Mark's problem. Over time, Mark's lack of flexibility when it comes to making changes in lifestyle and his difficulty in taking initiative could result in serious tension. Hannah has inner planets in H9, which will create a restlessness for new impressions, if she can but release them from the Pluto–Saturn opposition which dominates her natal chart.

It will be apparent, of course, that Mark's Pluto and Saturn falling so close to this conjunction in Hannah's chart are simply lending their weight by blending with this obstructive and difficult conjunction, which is manifesting in her life as control and constraint from the mores of the family and her locality. Her relationship with Mark is making her even more disinclined to move away from the family set-up.

A couple who is roughly the same age will have their respective outer planets very close to one another's. The implications of this need to be considered.

Before we turn to Mark's chart to do the same exercise, let us consider the importance of Mark's Neptune, the planet that finds more ways into Hannah's energy field than any other planet.

Pisces is the sign on the cusp of Hannah's House of Relationship. It indicates that she requires another to bring Piscean energy and perspectives into her life in order to balance her Virgoan practicality and sense of dutifulness, which is in evidence in her relationship with her mother.

Mark is not Piscean, but his Neptune makes many harmonious aspects to planets and key points in Hannah's chart. This would seem to account for the sense of the couple's being in their own world, which is the impression created when Mark and Hannah are together. He has brought a sense of specialness into her life, which, to Hannah, is one of the prime requirements of her relationships. She tries to find it in her relationship with her mother.

But it has been noted that Mark's Neptune falls on Hannah's south node, indicating that this very sense of specialness could, by way of being a compensating factor, seal her into a way of being that, for developmental reasons, she needs to leave behind. As H4 is involved, it must be assumed that motherhood would put that seal in place. With her natal Neptune in H4–5, Hannah would try to make her own relationship with a child the mother–child ideal that eluded Hannah and her mother. The position of the south node indicates that this is a familiar, non-progressive ideal.

We will now do this exercise again to learn *how constructive the relationship is in helping Mark move off the Moon and get behind his Sun.*

To do this, we will review aspects to Mark's:

- Moon
- Sun
- Saturn
- Key points

Mark:

☽ ⊼ ☽   ☉ □ ☉   ☿ ⊐ ♂   ♀ ⚹ ♃   ♂ ⚹ ♃   ♃ ∠ ♄   ♆ ⚹ ♇

☽ ⚹ ☿   ☿ □ ♄   ♀ ⚹ ⛢   ♂ ⚹ ⛢   ♃ ⚺ ⛢

☽ ⚹ ♂

☽ △ ♄

☽ ☍ ♆

☽ △ ♇

M △ ♀   Ⓐ ♐ ♀   ☊ ♐ ☉

M □ ☉   Ⓐ ⚺ ☉   ⊗ ♐ ♇

- Total number of conjunctions with Hannah's planets: 2
  - Harmonious: 0
  - Stressful: 2
- Total number of harmonious aspects received from Hannah's planets: 12
- Total number of stressful aspects received from Hannah's planets: 6

Closest aspects (not more than 1 degree orb).

☽ △ ♇

☉ □ ☉

⊗ ♐ ♇

1. An examination of aspects to the Moon reveals the following:

   - The injunct aspect between the two moons of Mark and Hannah has already been noted.
   - Apart from this, the many other aspects that Mark's Moon receives are harmonious, except for the opposition from Neptune, which indicates that what Hannah wishes to give to him may not be what he wants. This point should be considered in reference to the fact

that Hannah's Neptune is on the cusp of H4 and H5 (and that, in a woman's chart, this frequently indicates an idealized perception of motherhood) and that, natally, Mark has Uranus in H7.

- The large number of contacts made to Mark's Moon indicates that he relates to Hannah from a place of memory. The close trine from Hannah's Pluto will challenge this memory to some degree and enable his emotional response to be changed by present realities.

- Although Saturn casts a trine, any contact from this planet to the Moon is sobering. Here, it indicates that Mark feels emotionally constrained to some degree by Hannah's Saturn problem. Saturn in Scorpio is notoriously ungenerous, materially and emotionally, and uses a withholding strategy to remain in control. It must be assumed that this tendency is in Hannah's family and has shaped Hannah's own emotional nature. The square from Hannah's Saturn to Mark's Mercury should also be noted. Although the couple are always in communication, it is evident, even to observers, that it is Hannah (who has Mercury in Aries) doing the talking. Mark says very little. Maybe he (with Mercury in the restrained sign of Capricorn) cannot get a word in edgeways, or maybe Hannah talks as much as she does to compensate for his lack of input. Appearances can be deceptive. The conjunction made between Mark's Jupiter and Hannah's Saturn should also be noted. This has a very repressive effect upon the Jupiter person.

2. An examination of the aspects to the Sun reveals the following:

- The only contact that Mark's Sun receives is a challenging square from Hannah's Sun, which, as noted above in connection with Hannah, indicates incompatibility in the matter of life direction. This dearth of contacts that Mark's Sun may receive is a point of considerable significance, especially when viewed against the many contacts received by his Moon. This indicates that, for Mark, the relationship owes much to memory and is less directly helpful to him in the matter of moving on than it is to Hannah. This kind of discrepancy in a relationship is not at all uncommon. Mark's inner planets, with the exception of his Moon, receive significantly fewer aspects than Hannah's.

3. An examination of Mark's Saturn reveals the following:

- No contact from any of Hannah's outer planets, which indicates that the relationship does not challenge him or thereby open up new opportunities in the way it does for Hannah.

4. An examination of the key points reveals the following:

- Beneficent contacts from Hannah's Venus to the MC and, more potently, the Ascendant, which creates a tie of great affection and encouragement.
- Less positive is Hannah's Sun, which squares Mark's Ascendant and is conjunct with his north node. This is an outstanding indication of a personality (the Sun person) who will pull the node person back into an old way of being.
- Equally telling is the conjunction between Mark's Part of Fortune and Hannah's Saturn (orb of less than 2 degrees) and Pluto (exact). Mark and Hannah have come together so that he can, with assistance from Hannah's Pluto, work through yearning that has brought him back into incarnation. Pluto is a destructive planet: here, it indicates that, eventually, this relationship has to bring emotional turmoil into Mark's life to enable him to get free.

Summary

In looking at the relationship from Mark's point of view, it is evident that his relationship with Hannah is based largely on memory. The harsh truth is that, apart from creating an opportunity for him to pay something back through her (see references to Neptune) and to work through yearning, this relationship does not promote Mark's development in any direct way at all.

It is less that Hannah herself is a problem. It is more that Mark's present lifestyle, fashioned on his father's example, is not yet right for him. His relationship with Hannah is helping to make him feel comfortable and loved in circumstances from which, eventually, he has to move on, if Uranus in H7 is not to take matters into its own hands.

Mark's natal Saturn in H6 speaks of an old pattern of subservience to the needs and expectations of others. Mark, in his early twenties, is still a consummate 'fitter-in'.

Hannah could help them both if she were to insist that they move away, but Hannah has no real power over Mark in the form of an ability to challenge his way of looking at life. He is much better able to perform this role for her. Also, even though it is she who is the one more likely to think in such terms, he is unlikely to agree to it. Mark wants to keep things as they are, neither moving forwards into a greater formal commitment with Hannah (which he instinctively fears) nor moving away from his family – a piece of Libran indecision that will probably eventually cost him the relationship. When it works through H7, Uranus uses agents. Hannah's Uranus falls in Mark's H7 and blends its influence with his own. She most probably will leave him, quite abruptly, because he will not marry her and start a family. He will have his freedom thrust upon him, as most people with Uranus in H7 and H8 do.

No astrologer with any experience assesses the value of anything until he or she has seen the evidence for him- or herself. And the evidence shows that Hannah, who still has to let those H9 planets breathe and vivify her life, is deeply involved with a young man who has yet to get the measure of himself and his life.

Although in some part of ourselves we may wish for two people who are so obviously harmonious together to live happily ever after, we now know that if they do so, in the longer term it stands to be at the price of their developmental opportunities. This relationship is giving both Hannah and Mark an excuse to stay in the very circumstances that they need to leave behind.

Endnotes

1. In this area, less may be more. The more abstruse aspects do not add much to the understanding of the *point* of a relationship, but students should check out this matter for themselves.
2. Obviously, synastry is a factor in teaching and working with clients. In both situations, squares involving Mercury cause very real communication difficulties.
3. The British astrologer Sepharial claims that a mutual trine between the Sun and Moon is the best possible indicator of 'marital felicity'. In twenty years of practice, this author has never found such a configuration in any charts examined synastrically!

Chapter 8

The Lesson of Saturn, Chiron, and the Outer Planets

Introduction

The key word to describe a relating experience is *opportunity*. But each party does not experience opportunity in the same way. The person whose inner planet or planets are involved has the chance of a more conscious learning experience. For the outer-planet person, the real choice is to learn from the consequences of his or her actions, as he or she is the one with the energy that is expressing itself through him or her. He or she is identified with it and will usually only see it when the other holds up the mirror.

Although the Promoters provide the top line in a relationship and give it its appeal, or lack of it, benefitting the personalities involved, it is the outer planets which express the developmental possibilities of the relationship. In doing so, they set up often very challenging situations in relationships.

When the outer planets are acting as distributors into the chart of another, then a change of consciousness is required in the expression of the energy principles represented by the contacted planet and in the area of life where the faster-moving planet is placed. It is a learning situation, and, like all learning situations, it can take time and cause much pain.

The personality-focused idea of reincarnation, which the West has taken from the East and embroidered, has found a very rich vein to tap vis-à-vis the idea that people who have known each other in a past life are meant to reconnect in this lifetime.

The esotericist knows that personalities are always new, but our psyches are repositories of memories (old material) that we are processing through in light of our experiences in incarnation, including those brought about through our relationships. The soul, which provides continuity, supervises this process through the provision of learning opportunities that are built into the design of a life, including those that take the form of experiences in relationship.

- When Saturn is the distributor, the lesson is to come by greater awareness, sense of responsibility, and attention to detail.
- When Chiron is the distributor, the lesson is to face up to the spiritual implications of the tensions experienced.

- When Uranus is the distributor, the lesson is to loosen up and let go.
- When Neptune is the distributor, the lesson is to learn to give and make sacrifices.
- When Pluto is the distributor, the lesson is to clear the consciousness of old attitudes and assumptions that can no longer support development.

The outer planets determine the kind of experience that two personalities will have when they meet together. *What is not predetermined is what each party will make of the experience.* For example, Saturn will always bind, but what each party makes of the experience of being bound to another will depend, to a considerable extent, upon the degree of consciousness present, the mores of each person's culture, and the extent of each person's interest in spirituality.

- Be aware that whenever a slower-moving planet contacts a planet in another's chart, it will activate the natal theme connected with that planet (i.e. contact from another's Saturn will activate the Saturnian issue in the quesited's own chart).
- Always consider the area(s) of life (houses) in which both the faster- and slower-moving planets involved in contact are the significators, because this will reveal the circumstances through which this process is working.

Saturn

When Saturnian contact is a feature of the energy exchange between two people, learning through meeting with resistance is involved. Sometimes, this is confined simply to the energy principle represented by the planet and the area of life hosting the contact. But on other occasions, this aspect will dominate the synastry and set the tone of the relationship. The overall synastric picture will decide this.

Saturn as Distributor

This contact is evidence of a karmic need to focus upon the energy expressed through the planet which is contacted by Saturn. This is achieved through the difficulties and discomforts associated with attempts to express the contact in the relationship.

When the inner planets in one chart are contacted by aspect by Saturn in the chart of the other party, the result is almost always a sense of unease and heaviness on the part of the person whose inner planet(s) is (or are) so contacted. Yet, that person rarely moves him- or herself out of range. Soon, this sense of heaviness becomes a feature of the impact of that person. In its own way, it is taken as evidence of the significance of the relationship. On some level, the inner-planet person acknowledges the need to do better in his or her expression of this energy and usually tries very hard for a very long time, which, because the Saturn party is inflexible, produces the same result as a moth's battering itself against a light bulb. During this time, the two people are bound together.

Even when the trine or sextile aspect is involved, the inner-planet person will be aware of the sobering effect of the other. When the semi-square or square is involved, the Saturn person may be vocal in support of the stance that his or her Saturn recommends. He or she may also be critical or judgemental, to some degree.

The person whose Saturn is involved may be quite oblivious to this, as Saturn represents a habitual approach to life.

In synastry, Saturn is associated with durability and longevity. Sometimes, especially in the present day, the person whose inner planet(s) is (or are) involved will eventually rebel and fight for freedom, either to express that energy uncensored or to move on from the relationship itself.

The effect of this kind of stance in the relationship is marked. It is as if a switch has been flicked. The Saturn person misses the impact of the exchange so much that he or she moves from being the resistant, critical party to become the pursuer. This may be the first time that the individual really becomes aware of the importance of this connection, which he or she may have sacrificed to inflexibility and lack of awareness. When this person becomes the pursuer, it is usually too late to restore the relationship. The lesson has been learned by the person for whom it was designed.

- Look out for the conjunction aspect in the charts of those who commit to significantly older partners. The conjunction aspect is also found in the charts of children who are overshadowed by successful parents, particularly fathers. When the father is often physically or emotionally absent from the family, there is opposition.
- Look out for squares between Saturn and Mercury in cases where one party claims not to be heard by the other; and between Saturn and Venus where one party feels consistently rejected and unappreciated by the other.

Saturn as Recipient

Such contact is evidence of a developmental need to be released from the limitations of a habitual perspective. Often, a lack of responsibility or discrimination is in evidence.

When Saturn is contacted by the outer planets, the Saturn person feels fear because he or she knows that the defences he or she relies upon are under attack, as indeed they are when the contact attempts to release the person from the limitations of a habitual approach to life. The Saturn person may or may not understand why this should be happening or what the benefits might be, but he or she always knows that it *is* happening and knows that the other party is responsible for it. Therefore, the individual reacts to this as Saturn itself dictates. These contacts produce much negative and fearful behaviour.

Chiron

When this contact is a feature of the energy exchange between two people, the learning comes through experiencing a situation familiar from past life and reintroduced through contact with the other party. This exposes attitudes and assumptions that have become an obstacle to spiritual development.

Chiron as Distributor

When Chiron contacts the inner and superior planets or key points in the chart of another, it creates spiritually testing situations for that person so that he or she may develop a new understanding in relation to it. The effect of this contact is almost always a sense of tension and spiritual anxiety on the part of the person whose inner planet(s) is (or are) so contacted. The degree of the tension will be determined by the nature of the aspect.

The contact between two people does not need to be sustained. Even if they move apart, the issue has been reopened, making it so that the person whose inner planets are involved cannot escape it. The desirable outcome is always a shift in consciousness and a release from uncertainty and confusion in respect of the principle represented by the planet that Chiron contacts and also by the Chiron problem revealed (by sign and house position) through the quesited's chart.

Such contacts have piquancy without being amongst the heavyweights of synastry. Undoubtedly, this owes much to the fact that, consciously or unconsciously, the Chiron person acts as the healer/teacher. This, of itself, is not an inimical role to the personality.

Chiron as Recipient

When Chiron is contacted by outer planets, the effect is disturbing to the Chiron person who knows that he or she is defenceless against the attack upon this sore place of his or her consciousness. The person's only real choice is to cooperate the best he or she can with the process over which he or she has no control. The nature of that process will be determined by the quality of the outer planet.

Uranus

When Uranian contact is a feature of the energy exchange between two people, the developmental opportunity is to move on from the limitation of old thought structures and emotional patterns.

Sometimes, this is confined simply to the energy principle represented by the planet. On other occasions, this aspect dominates the synastry and is the dominant note of the relationship. Again, the overall synastric picture will decide this.

Uranus as Distributor

Such contact is evidence of a karmic need to free up by breaking attachments and becoming less rigid and more experimental.

When the inner planets in one chart are contacted by aspect by Uranus in the chart of the other party, the result is almost always a sense of excitement and freneticism. Life seems to speed up. The person whose inner planet is involved in the contact feels inspired by the other's way of handling that energy principle, if not by the other's lifestyle as a whole, because it seems so much bolder and freer.

What is rarely on offer when Uranus is strong in the synastry is stability. The Uranian person, having a karmic need to break an attachment to the other party, is not available for commitment in that relationship, even if the Uranian person may not have consciously arrived at this realisation. Because Uranus works without the consent of the conscious mind, the Uranian person may have no understanding of how it is that his or her own energy is responsible for the failure of the relationship to gel.

Understandably, this can cause much distress to both parties. Ironically, in such a situation, it is often easier for the party whose inner planet is contacted to deal with the situation, as he or she eventually rationalises about the other's inability to commit and thereby cuts his or her losses.

When Uranus makes contact from a harmonious angle, the situation is much lighter than when it involves a stressful aspect. When the conjunction is involved, the relationship usually takes off like a whirlwind with nowhere to go.

- Look out for a harmonious aspect between Uranus and Venus in the synastry of couples who repeatedly break up and get back together without ever moving the relationship on.
- Look out for stressful synastric aspects of Uranus to the Sun or Moon when a child has a difficult relationship with the parent and the two cannot bond.

Uranus as Recipient

When Uranus is contacted by Neptune or Pluto, the effect upon the Uranian person occurs below the threshold of consciousness and operates, as it were, behind the scenes of the relationship. The Uranian person is unlikely to make a connection between the other party and this process – of which he or she will be only vaguely aware, in any case.

Neptune

When Neptunian contact is a feature of the energy exchange between two people, the developmental opportunity is to move out from a selfish, defensive perspective and open up emotionally.

Neptune as Distributor

When Neptune contacts inner and superior planets or key points, the effect is a powerful emotional response that may not be obviously sexual, even when it involves two people who are partner material.

For the person whose inner planets are contacted, it is an opportunity to experience loving and giving that may erode negative attitudes or inflexibility.

The Neptune person has a karmic need to give something to the other to discharge a debt. The nature of that donation can be deduced from the planet involved in the contact and from the sign and house position of Neptune in the distributor's chart.

The harmonious aspects make this state of affairs more sustainable and more balanced. With the conjunction, the effect can be sublime, involving out-of-body experiences and a powerful psychic connection. With the stressful aspects, delusion, misunderstanding, and poor communication are likely to be a factor in the response of both parties

- Look out for harmonious synastric aspects of Neptune and the Moon when two people fit together as though they have always known each other.
- Look out for stressful synastric aspects between Neptune and Mercury when clear communication with another person seems impossible to achieve, and between Neptune and Venus when two people will not acknowledge their obvious incompatibility.
- Look out for harmonious synastric aspects of Neptune and Jupiter when one person introduces spirituality in a meaningful way to another.

Neptune as Recipient

Neptune can be received only from Pluto. The result of this contact is to step up the transformative effect of being able to move beyond personality perspectives in the area of life in which Neptune is found. Owing to the slow movement of both these planets, the range of aspects that can form between one person's Neptune and another's Pluto is very limited, even when the synastric review involves people from different generations.

Pluto

When Pluto is a feature of the energy exchange between two people, the relationship is an agent of transformation in a very uncompromising way. In this case, both parties need to be aware of the value of having issues, with which they would rather not deal, come up forcibly between them. Understandably, few are.

Pluto as Distributor

When the inner and superior planets or key points in one person's chart are contacted by Pluto in the chart of the other, the effect is challenging. The developmental opportunity is to arrive at a deeper understanding of the energy principle involved in the contact.

The Pluto person has a karmic need to externalise tendencies that are in his or her psyche in order to become aware of them, to face the truth, and to gain a more complete understanding of him- or herself. This is most likely to happen *after* his or her behaviour has produced a reaction or stance from the other party who, thereby, has provided a mirror in which the person can see him- or herself. Until then, the individual is likely to be unaware of it: he or she is simply being him- or herself.

When the harmonious aspects are involved, the situation is more comfortable, and the need for it is more readily appreciated by the person whose inner planets are so contacted. Of itself, the contact creates intensity in a relationship, especially in connection with the energy principle represented by the contact planet, but it is not necessarily destabilizing.

When the stressful aspects are concerned, the controlling behaviour of the Pluto person may be too much for the other party. When Pluto is contacting the Moon, Venus, or Mars, especially in conjunction aspect, physical or emotional violence is common. In any event, the Pluto person will deliver a profound shock to the other party and be him or herself shocked by what he or she is capable of. This is not always a negative realisation: a person who has denied his or her own power may reconnect with it through the agency of Pluto.

- Look out for the stressful aspects between Pluto and the Moon in cases of child abuse and domestic violence, and between Pluto, Venus, and Mars in vengeful relationships.
- Look out for synastric aspects (usually harmonious) between Pluto and Jupiter when one party changes the belief system and outlook of the other.

Synastry Postscript: Hannah, Mark, and Everyman

For our grandparents' generation, economic and social necessities encouraged an attitude that is well summed up in the expression 'We've made our bed, now we must lay on it.' Also, the door was shut tight on a close examination of the dynamics between the two people. Our parents' generation began to show an interest in what was behind the door. Our generation has thrown open the door to let in Uranus, the principle of individuation. The result, for sure, is not greater stability or easier relationships. Neither Mark nor Hannah comes from a background that questions the idea that if you find the right person, you stick with that person for life, because the relationship will be meeting all the basic requirements. Already, although only in their early twenties, Mark and Hannah's lives and opportunities are being shaped by the relationship. Almost certainly, Hannah is shutting out the pain and, probably, panic that she is experiencing because Mark will not talk marriage. He is allowing himself to be fenced by his desire to preserve the status quo. His sense that marriage would change things is probably an illusion because he is committed. What they have is a deep affection. Each has someone on whom to rely, but it is not easy to see where their lives together are going, as they are both compromising in areas that are important to their development. But they are of their generation. Big changes are needed. They can change either together or separately. But whatever the future holds, their time together has enriched them both. In some respects, it would be better for them to quit before diminishing returns set in, but this is not the way people are in matters of the heart. It is for this reason that Uranus has become so busy in our lives and relationships. As we have let it in, maybe, in time, we will learn to understand and cooperate better with the work that it does on behalf of our development.

Part Three

The Relationship Itself - Compository

Chapter 9

Compository – Shifting the Focus

1. Introduction

Compository presupposes the fact of relationship. The technique will reveal little about the history of the involvement; and, its longevity is something that will have to be deduced. It will not show whether a relationship between two people who barely know each other will develop into something other than it is, but, rather, if it should, what will be the features of the association. Nor is a composite chart the place to look for the developmental significance or the quality of a relationship, as far as each partner is concerned. These aspects belong to the province of synastry.

The function of compository is to show how the energies of two people, when blended in a relationship, will express themselves.

A composite chart can be created for any two people, provided that one has the relevant birth data – but they may never meet. The chart itself would not show this because it *presupposes* the fact of relationship. And so there would be no point to the exercise.

Compository becomes meaningful when circumstance has brought two people together on some level, not necessary physical, and when they are both aware of the relationship and have the expectation that it will be an established feature of their lives. Their relationship to each other can be of any kind: kin, friends, lovers, business colleagues. The chart will show the optimum use of their pooled resources, but not how to handle the dynamics of the relationship itself.

But, once drafted, a composite chart may then be assessed (using the technique of synastry) against the natal charts of the individuals concerned to see what the reality of each makes of the purpose of the relationship of which he or she is a part.

Generally speaking, people concerned with their relationship want to know how to make it work better and are less concerned with how to direct it. Yet, if a relationship is encouraged to express itself in the way that it lends itself, then it can be assumed that it will work more smoothly because it will be purposeful, not in terms of the purpose of the individual but in terms of the relationship itself.

This is a way of thinking in which, generally speaking, we are not practised, but, in fact, it is of the nature of soul consciousness, which is inclusive of its constituents and is focused upon them. Compository requires a shift of focus because it deals with the third aspect of relating, with the unit of consciousness made by the coming together of two people on some level, and by what the relationship will give to the world. Usually, the technique reveals more than people who have conventional expectations of relationship want to have to consider.

Compository yields up fascinating information, but it is hard work. Computer software is not much help. Most of the routine calculations will have to be done manually.

2. Overview of the Technique of Compository

A composite chart is created from the midpoint of the positions of a planet in two charts. For example, using the charts of Hannah and Mark:

- The Sun in their composite chart will be at Pisces 2 degrees, 4 minutes, which is the midpoint between their two placements *by the shortest route*.
- The Moon in their composite chart will be at Libra 15 degrees, 34 minutes, which is the midpoint between their two placements *by the shortest route*.

This method is applied to all of the planets in turn. Although the mathematics may be rather tedious if the exercise is undertaken manually, there is nothing controversial about this.

However, compository does have its controversial areas.

I.   Using the midpoint method, it is possible that, in the composite chart, the inner planets (Mercury and Venus) may create astronomically impossible positions to the Sun.

For example, Mercury, because of the nature of its orbit, can never be more than 28 degrees away from the Sun. But, in the composite chart, the position of Mercury derived from the midpoint of Mercury in two charts can put it at a distance from the composite chart Sun, which exceeds what is astronomically possible.

How are we to think about this?

The composite chart is derivative; it is a secondary document (the primary documents are the natal charts). Compository looks at the possibilities in the blending of energies – at an open-ended situation, *not at a moment in time*. Such a moment in time would be the first meeting. A primary document could be created for this. The composite chart is an effect of that first meeting, but it stands outside time.

It is for each astrologer to decide whether he or she feels that a secondary document should reflect the astronomical realities of a birth chart. If there is unease about creating a composite chart in which Mercury and Venus may have an astronomically invalid relationship to the

Sun, then the inner planets should be calculated in a different way, which would involve using the average of the aspect between the Sun and Mercury in the two natal charts.

Let us consider this with reference to Hannah and Mark's composite Mercury.

The midpoint method puts Mercury at Pisces 16 degrees, 5 minutes, which is within 28 degrees of the Sun and, in this case, is astronomically possible.

But if we are wary of the fact that this might not be the case, then, using the average distance method – which makes 15 degrees, 29 minutes the average distance of Hannah and Mark's Mercurys from their Suns – we see that the position of composite Mercury is 17 degrees, 33 minutes.

Students are advised to work with both methods until they get a feel for what is the better method.

We will go through the calculation for this in the next chapter.

II. The matter of how to set the house frame from a composite chart, like most matters involving houses, is one on which there is little consensus.

The principal variations are these:

1. Calculating the midpoint of the two Ascendants as shown in the natal chart and using the Equal House method to establish the remaining house cusps.
2. Calculating the MC by the method given above and using the Equal House method to establish the other house cusps, *including the Ascendant*.
3. Deriving the MC from the midpoint and using a table of houses for the latitude of the place in which the couple are living in order to ascertain the remaining cusps. The obvious drawback to this is that they may not be living in the same place.
4. Deriving the MC from the midpoints and then using a table of houses for the latitude of the place where the couple met. The obvious drawback, especially in these days of Internet chat rooms, is that the people may not have met in a physical location.
5. Use different methods to suit different situations. Unsatisfactory though this may initially sound, consider that a relationship in which there is no physical contact will be of a different nature and quality from one in which there is. Why should the methodology not reflect this? (See endnote 1.)

Compository is not for people who are new to astrology but for those who have a respect for and understanding of the way in which the language of astrology can validly accommodate the differing perspective of those who use it.

Figure C

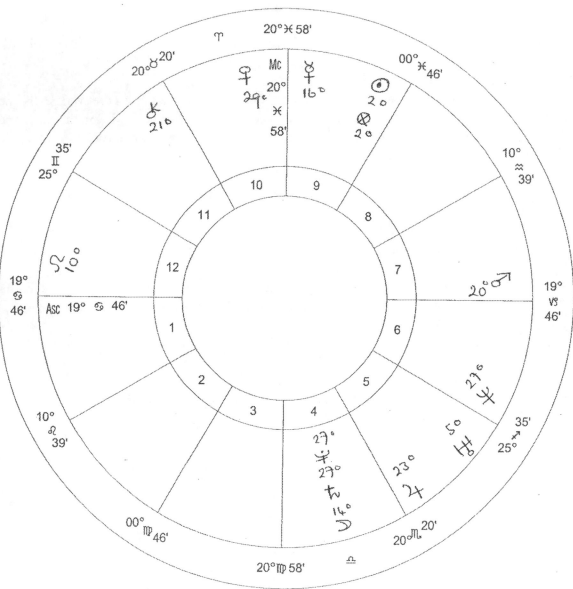

Hannah and Mark: composite chart
Geocentric, Tropical, Koch house system
©Winstar Matrix software

Figure D

Hannah: a synastric comparison with the composite chart
Geocentric, Tropical, Koch house system
©Winstar Matrix software

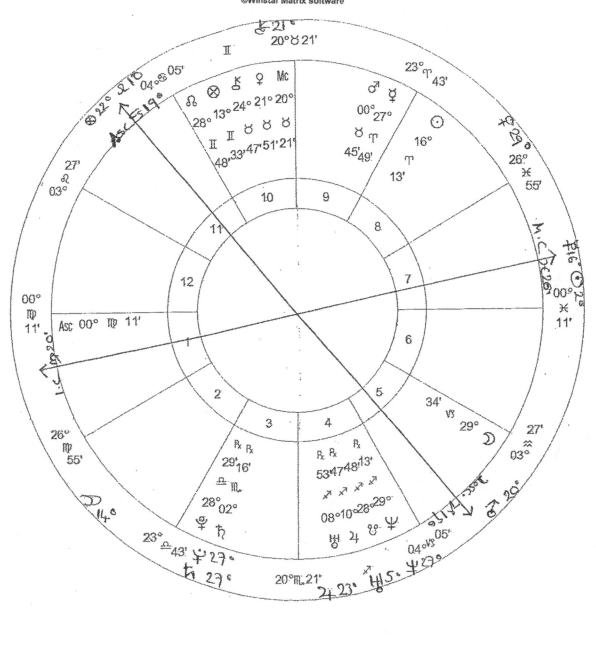

Figure E

Mark: a synastric comparison with the composite chart
Geocentric, Tropical, Koch house system
©Winstar Matrix software

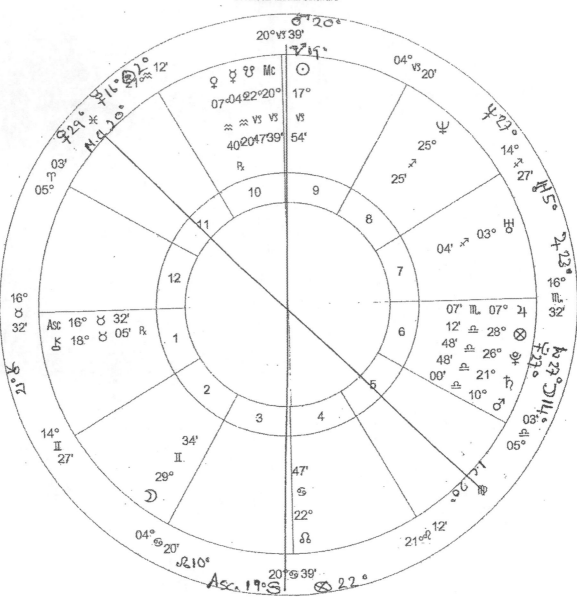

Figure D, Aspects: Hannah and the Composite Chart

	☉	☽	☿	♀	♂	♃	♄	⚷	♅	♆	♇	Asc	Mc	⊗	☊
☉		⚼			✶		△		□	✶	△	☍			
☽	□				✶										
☿	⚼			✶											
♀		✶	⚼		⚼		⚻	✶		□	⚻	⚻			
♂	□			△			△						△		
♃		⚻	✶						☍				☍		
♄		□	□					⚻		☌					
⚷				☌			☌						☌		
♅		✶				☌	⚼		☌			ASC			
♆		⚼	△		✶		⚻				✶		⚼		☌
♇		□	□				⚻			☌					
Asc	□			✶											
Mc				△											
⊗															
☊															

Figure E, Aspects: Mark and the Composite Chart

	☉	☽	☿	♀	♂	♃	♄	⚷	♅	♆	♇	Asc	Mc	⊗	☊
☉	∠	△	⚼			△			□						
☽	□				☌										
☿	✶						✶						✶		
♀			□						△	□					
♂	☌						□	△					☌		☍
♃	✶						⚼	☍					✶		✶
♄		△						⚻		✶	☌			☌	
⚷	△							☌							
♅	∠		✶	✶	✶				☌				∠		
♆		☍								☌					
♇		△					☌			✶	☌				
Asc	☍						□	✶							
Mc	✶						⚻	✶							
⊗							□						☍		☌
☊					□										

Endnote

1. This lack of consensus should not be off-putting to the student with astrological experience who, after all, has found a way through the house systems controversy and has probably forgotten that it was ever an issue. Use the method that appeals most, but also experiment with the others, using your own chart and those of people with whom you have had contact of different kinds.

    In situations in which a couple have never physically met, the author favours the method that derives the MC from the midpoint and uses the Equal House method to put the other house cusps, including the Ascendant, in place.

    If the people have met, then deriving the MC from the midpoint of the two MCs and using a table of houses for the latitude of the place in which they met is recommended. This way, the birth of the relationship is represented in the chart.

    Deriving the MC, rather than the Ascendant, from the midpoint is logical because compository concerns the purpose to which the relationship can be put, where it can go, and what it can give out. These matters to relate to the MC.

Chapter 10

The Technique of Compository

1. Getting Organised for a Composite Chart

To draft a composite chart, the birth data of the individuals is required. As is ever the case in exercises involving the natal chart, the more accurate the data, the more reliable the results.

For sure, there are computer programmes that give composite placements for the planets, but the software for compository is not included in packages as commonly as are other kinds of astrological charts.

If drafting the chart manually, the most time-consuming aspect of the exercise will be the calculation of the planets' places. This will be assisted by the use of a chart which converts the signs into numerical values:

Aries: 0 (or 12)
Taurus: 1
Gemini: 2
Cancer: 3
Leo: 4
Virgo: 5
Libra: 6
Scorpio: 7
Sagittarius: 8
Capricorn: 9
Aquarius: 10
Pisces: 11

Thus, Hannah's Sun at Aries 16 13 becomes 0 16 13. Mark's Sun at Capricorn 17 54 becomes 9 17 54.

2. Calculating the Planets' Places

When calculating the midpoints, always use the shortest distance between the planets in question. When applying the result of the calculation, *add* if moving in the direction of the signs, or *subtract* if going against it, which is the case if moving from Aries through Pisces.

The Composite Sun

The shortest distance between the two suns is represented by moving from Aries to Capricorn through Pisces: 0 16 13.

To make the sum easier: 12 16 13

                                      09 17 54

                                      02 28 19

Divide this result:

2 28 19

  2

= 1 14 10

Add this result to the placement of Mark's Sun (or subtract from Hannah's Sun):

9 17 54 +

1 14 10

11 02 04

Read this back:

The sign Pisces has the numerological value 11, and so the midpoint is Composite Sun: Pisces 2 degrees, 4 minutes.

This needs to be done for all planets.

Moon

Hannah: 9 29 34 –

Mark: 2 29 34

                 7 00 00 / divide by 2

                 3 15 00 +

                 2 29 34

                 6 14 34

Composite Moon: Libra 14 degrees, 34 minutes

Mercury

As the midpoint:

Hannah: 00 27 49 or 12 27 49 –
Mark: <u>10 04 20</u>
                    2 23 29 / divide by 2

                 01 11 45 +
                 <u>10 04 20</u>
                 11 16 05

Composite Mercury: Pisces 16 degrees, 5 minutes

Alternative method – as average distance of Mercury from Sun:

Hannah: distance of Mercury from Sun = 14 degrees, 32 minutes (in advance of Sun)
Mark: distance of Mercury from Sun = 16 degrees, 26 minutes (in advance of Sun)

= 14 32 +
    <u>16 26</u>
    30 58

Therefore, average distance is <u>30 58</u>   15 29 in advance of the Sun, so add result
                          2

Composite Sun   Pisces   02 04 +
                          <u>15 29</u>

         Composite Mercury: Pisces 17 degrees, 33 minutes (see endnote 1)

Venus

As the midpoint:

Hannah: 01 21 51 or 13 21 51 –
Mark: <u>10 07 40</u>
          03 14 11 / divide by 2

=   01 22 06 +
                  <u>10 07 40</u>
                  11 29 46

= Pisces 29 degrees, 46 minutes

Alternative method – as average distance of Venus from Sun

Hannah: distance of Venus from Sun = 34 degrees, 48 minutes (in advance of Sun)
Mark: distance of Mercury from Sun = 19 degrees, 46 minutes (in advance of Sun)

=   34 48 +
      19 46
      54 34

Therefore, the average distance is <u>54 34</u> = 27 17 in advance of the Sun, so add result.

Composite Sun   Pisces 02 04 +
                         <u>27 17</u>

Composite Venus: Pisces 29 degrees, 21 minutes

Mars

Hannah 01 00 45 or   13 00 45
Mark   <u>06 10 00</u>
                        06 20 45 / divide by 2

          03 10 23 +
          <u>06 10 00</u>
          09 20 23

Composite Mars: Capricorn 20 degrees, 23 minutes

Jupiter

Hannah: 08 10 47 −
Mark: <u>07 07 07</u>
            01 03 40 / divide by 2

            00 16 50 +
            <u>07 07 07</u>
            07 23 57

Composite Jupiter: Scorpio 23 degrees, 57 minutes

Saturn

Hannah: 07 02 16 –
Mark: <u>06 21 48</u>
             00 10 28 / divide by 2

             00 05 14 +
             <u>06 21 48</u>
             06 27 02

        Composite Saturn: Libra 27 degrees, 2 minutes

Chiron

Hannah: 01 24 47 -
Mark: <u>01 18 05</u>
             00 06 42 / divide by 2

             00 03 21 +
             <u>01 18 05</u>
             01 21 26

        Composite Chiron: Taurus 21 degrees, 26 minutes

Uranus

Hannah: 08 08 53 –
Mark: <u>08 03 04</u>
             00 05 49 / divide by 2

             00 02 55 +
             <u>08 03 04</u>
             08 05 59

        Composite Uranus: Sagittarius 5 degrees, 59 minutes

Neptune

Hannah: 08 29 13 –
Mark: <u>08 25 25</u>
             00 03 48 / divide by 2

             00 01 54 +
             <u>08 25 25</u>
             08 27 19

        Composite Neptune: Sagittarius 27 degrees, 19 minutes

Pluto

Hannah: 06 28 29 -
Mark: 06 26 48
             00 01 41 / divide by 2

=   00 00 5l +
             06 26 48
             06 27 39

Composite Pluto: Libra: 27 degrees, 39 minutes

3. Calculating Additional Features

i)   The nodes

The north node should be ascertained as the planets' placements have been calculated, i.e. using the midpoint of the two natal placements.

The south node, obviously, is the polar opposite point.
Mark: 3 22 47 –
Hannah: 2 28 48
             0 23 59

0 23 59
   2

= 0 11 59

Add to placement of Hannah's north node:

2 28 59 +
0 11 59
3 10 58

- Composite North Node: Cancer 10 degrees, 58 minutes
- Composite South Node: Capricorn 10 degrees, 58 minutes

ii) The Part of Fortune

The Part of Fortune should be calculated from the composite placements of the Sun, Moon, and Ascendant:

Composite Moon:	6 14 34
Composite Ascendant:	<u>3 19 57 +</u>
	10 04 31 =
Composite Sun:	<u>11 02 04 –</u>
	11 02 23 =

Composite Part of Fortune: Pisces 2 degrees, 23 minutes

3. The House Frame

Having calculated the planets' places, the next task is to construct the house frame.

As Hannah and Mark have physically met, we will construct the house frame from the midpoint of their MCs and use a table of houses from Brighton (UK), where they met, to ascertain the house cusps.

Hannah's MC is Taurus 20 21.
Mark's MC is Capricorn 20 39.

The shortest distance between the two MCs is 01.
20 21 1 = 13 20 21 –
       <u>09 20 39</u>
       03 29 42

<u>03 29 42</u>
  2

= 01 29 51

Add this result to Mark's MC:

09 20 39 +
<u>01 29 51</u>
11 20 30

Composite MC: Pisces 20 degrees, 30 minutes

Brighton is latitude 50 degrees 50 minutes.

At 23 hours, 24 minutes, 00 seconds, Pisces 20 degrees, 21 minutes, is on the MC. This is sufficiently accurate.

In this exercise, we have no use for the time heading the table, so disregard it. Simply use the degrees on the house cusps.

When Pisces 20 is on the MC at 50 degrees north, 50 minutes, the other house cusps are as follows.

MC ♓ 20	11	12	Ascendant	2	3
Koch	♉ 20	♊ 25	♋ 19 57	♌ 10	♍ 1
Placidus	♈ 28	♊ 13	♋ 19 57	♌ 6	♌ 25

The chart may now be constructed (see figure C).

Endnote

1. If one or both of the placements should be behind the Sun (i.e. later in the sign or in the following sign), then give this a *negative value* and proceed as shown above.

Chapter 11

Interpreting the Composite Chart

1. Introduction

In compository, we are dealing with the relationship between two people and with the thing that their coming together has created.

Compository shows to us how the coming together of two people creates opportunities that may take those people beyond their own individual realities. From a developmental point of view, this is the point of relationship.

At first, few students find it easy to adapt to the chart of an impersonal entity using the methods that they have learned to get to grips with a person's horoscope. And yet the process is essentially the same, *although there is no place for the esoteric rulerships when examining an impersonal entity.*

As is always the case in chart interpretation, take the initiative and create a structure for the inquiry.

But before doing this, let us first consider the tools that we will be using in our inquiry. It is recommended that students learn to use a small number of tools well, increasing their number as they find this beneficial.

The basic tools that are recommended are these:

1. The Sun
2. The MC–IC
3. The Ascendant–Descendant
4. The Moon
5. The Moon's nodes
6. The Part of Fortune

2. The Basic Tools

1. Purpose

i)   The Sun – the potential of the relationship

In compository, the Sun, by sign and house position, indicates the potential of the relationship, i.e. to what it will lend itself. Whether that will be realised will depend upon:

- The consciousness of the partners and their interest in the relationship's achieving its potential. When it comes to relationship, our thinking is heavily conditioned. There may be no interest in the relationship outside a small range of conventional criteria. The relationship of each of the partners to the relationship itself is something that may be studied using synastry.
- How long the relationship lasts may be a factor, but longevity is not necessarily the guarantor of potential realisation any more than its absence will automatically prevent the relationship from fulfilling its potential. *To a very considerable extent, this matter will be determined by the nature of that potential.* The longevity is something that has to be deduced from the relationship's inner dynamics.

ii) The MC (Midheaven) – The Contribution Made by the Relationship

The sign on the Midheaven indicates the nature of the contribution that the relationship is able to make, i.e. the kind of values it supports. As with its potential, indicated by the composite Sun, the extent to which it is able to make this contribution will depend upon the interest of the partners in permitting the relationship to express itself in this way; and that will depend, at least in part, on the relationship that each partner has to this kind of energy.

The sign on the IC indicates the kind of energy that the relationship relies upon for its own nourishment.

2. Consciousness

i)   The Ascendant–Descendant – the quality of the consciousness expressing itself through and attracted by the relationship

The Ascendant–Descendant axis is concerned with the quality of consciousness expressed through the relationship, including attitudes towards relating itself.

- The sign on the composite Ascendant and any planets in H1 will indicate the energy given out and the way that others experience it.
- The energy that the relationship attracts to itself is indicated by the sign on the Descendant and any planets in H7. This indicates the

quality of energy the relationship brings in through the interaction of the partners, as a couple, with other people.

ii) The Moon's nodes – developing consciousness through experience

The lunar nodes are concerned with the consciousness developed by experience within a form. In a composite chart, the form is the relationship itself.

- The Moon's north node indicates the kind of awareness that this relationship will develop on behalf of those involved in it, by virtue of their being in it. A study of the charts of the individuals involved will reveal the extent to which this awareness stands to assist the development of each.
- The south node indicates the values that have supported its formation.

3. Foundations

i) The Moon – the expectations of the relationship

In the composite chart, the Moon, by sign and house position, indicates the assumptions and expectations underpinning the relationship.

- Just as there may be conflict between an individual's true identity and his or her assumptions about his or her life, so a relationship will be strengthened or weakened by the extent to which the potential is supported or challenged by the assumptions brought to the relationship. This is something that may be deduced from the aspect between the Sun and the Moon.
- The extent to which the relationship is able to accommodate the expectation of each partner is something that will be revealed by from the synastric comparison.

ii) The IC – the energy that the relationship relies upon for its own nourishment

The energy and values associated with the sign on the IC will keep the relationship going. Deprived of them, the relationship is unlikely to survive because it is failing in its raison d'être, which is distinct from its purpose.

iii) Saturn – the area of challenge in the relationship

- As in the natal chart, Saturn in a composite chart indicates the area of life in which the relationship will receive challenges and where conscious, intelligent choices will have to be made. The problems arise from attitudes brought into the relationship.
- It may be that marriages which are legally structured arrangements may cope better with the Saturnian challenge than informal

arrangements will. Saturn is exalted in the sign Libra, which rules formalised relationships.

iv) The Part of Fortune – the raison d'être of the relationship

The Part of Fortune indicates the conscious or unconscious desires, which are the cause of the relationship's coming into being. This is something different from its purpose, which is future-oriented.

4. Structuring the Inquiry

With these basic tools, answers can be found to the following questions, which we will use to structure our inquiry:

- To what will the relationship lend itself?
- What are the assumptions upon which it was built, and to what extent will the relationship fulfil these assumptions?
- What are its inner strengths and weaknesses?
- How does it present itself to the world?
- How do others respond to it?

We will now look at what this means, using the composite chart of Hannah and Mark.

5. Interpretation

All standard considerations and disciplines of horoscopy are applicable when interpreting a composite exercise.

Although secondary and primary directions cannot meaningfully be used in conjunction with a composite chart because the composite chart represents a unit of consciousness rather than a moment in time, there is a form of progression based upon a predictive method called Mundane Directions that can be used to establish timings. Transit activity does apply. It must also be assumed that when a planet in the composite chart receives energy from a transiting planet, especially an outer planet, there will be a significant effect upon the relationship. We cover this matter in the Appendix.

Hannah and Mark: The Relationship Itself

1. Purpose / Intention

i)   The Sun – the potential of the relationship

In Pisces in H9, the composite Sun indicates that the relationship is supportive of expansiveness and that it stands for increasing understanding and transcending of narrow, conditioned ways of thinking.

The relationship is capable of giving Hannah and Mark a different way of understanding life and may take them overseas.

The presence of the Sun sign's rulers – Jupiter in Scorpio in H5 and Neptune in Sagittarius in H6 – indicates that these two areas of life (H5, creative expression, including sexual expression; H6, work) will be most obviously influenced by this expansive attitude.

- Supporting the Sun and therefore the relationship in its capacity as a vehicle of expansion for the two partners are trines from Saturn and Pluto, both in H4, which indicates that the relationship encapsulates a conscious need to move on from the past and from the standards of the families to which Hannah and Mark belong.
- Working against the Sun is a square from Uranus from H5. Uranus rules H8 and is located in H5. This indicates that influences from outside (i.e. other people) will seriously challenge the relationship, manifesting, in all probability, as 'extramarital' affairs. Uranus in square aspect to the Sun is a seriously destabilising factor in the relationship, and yet the nature of Uranus is such that it must be assumed that these challenges offer the relationship the opportunity to become stronger and more conscious of its purpose of transcending narrow and conditioned ways of thinking. Precisely who is likely to engage in the extramarital affairs may be evident from the synastric comparison, which we will undertake in the next lesson.

ii)   The Midheaven – the contribution made by the relationship

In the composite chart of Hannah and Mark, the sign Pisces appears on the MC, but it will be noted that the sign Aries is intercepted in H1 0.

The sign Pisces is, of course, passive/feminine and supports the idea that sacrifice is required on the part of those involved, not simply to comply with the wishes and needs of the other, but also to the conform to the expectations that society has of relationship. Pisces's rulers, Jupiter and Neptune, are found in H5 and H6, indicating the areas of life where sacrifice, tolerance, and flexibility will be most in evidence.

Supporting this passive, compliant stance is Mercury, ruling H3 and H12, which is in conjunction with the MC. Yet, the presence of Aries in H10 indicates that, in time, the relationship will support more proactive values and encourage a more dynamic attitude on the part of the two people involved. As Aries's ruler, Mars is in H7. This indicates that the change in energy will bring about a changed, more assertive way of functioning in and through relationship.

2. Consciousness

i)   The Ascendant–Descendant – the quality of the consciousness expressing itself through and attracted by the relationship

Together, Hannah and Mark express Cancerian energy, which is emotional, caring, and nurturing and is very much influenced by familial conditioning. Outsiders will be aware of this, and they may also be aware of a childlike quality in the relationship. Although they are now in their early twenties, Hannah and Mark got together as young teenagers and may still be seen by others as being young and inexperienced, which, in one sense, at least, they are. Neither has been out with anyone else. They may remain caught up in patterns that formed when they were both still at school. It is notable that they go and stay with Hannah's mother at weekends, which rather indicates that they do not feel that they have properly separated out from the parents or can invite Hannah's mother into their own world.

The energy that they attract is Capricornian: sober, supervising, disciplining, and structuring. Hannah's mother is Capricorn. The equilibrium of the relationship depends upon this. The extent of the influence of his father upon Mark's lifestyle has been noted.

- The Moon and Sun are in sesqui-quadrate aspect, indicating tension between the potential of the relationship and its reason for coming into being.
- The Moon, which is the ruling planet, is also square the Ascendant–Descendant from the sign Libra. The Moon, as the fastest-moving body amongst the planets in H4, is the recipient of the combined energy of Saturn and Pluto – which in H4 challenges the inheritance, especially that coming in through the mother. This indicates that this kind of consciousness and way of operating will come from within the relationship itself.

ii) The Moon's nodes – developing consciousness through experience

Regardless of how consciously and purposefully they conduct themselves in the relationship, Hannah and Mark, simply by being in the relationship, will become more emotionally aware, moving on from a way of looking at life that is largely materialistic and work-oriented. They will be required to consider larger issues, particularly the role of the family in the lives of individuals. Since the ruler of the north node is the Moon, described above as receiving the combined influence of Saturn and Pluto, it is to be expected that the (eventual) resistance to the traditional way of being in relationship, expressed by their families, will be an important factor for Mark and Hannah in this matter.

The fact that the north node is in H12 indicates that in undergoing this shift in consciousness, Hannah and Mark are helping to bring about change in the way their generation looks at the matter of family, expectations, and familial conditioning.

3. Foundations

i) The Moon – the expectations of the relationship

The Moon in the composite chart is in the sign Libra in H4. Throughout this book, the harmony that is in evidence between Hannah and Mark has been remarked upon. This smoothness and flow is a quality of Libra. The Moon indicates that the expectation is for the relationship to be a harmonious blending both of the two people involved and of the domestic environment. Hannah and Mark may be putting a lot of work into ensuring that their relationship is as smooth and equitable as they think it should be. As is always a possibility when the Moon is in Libra, that harmony may be preserved at the expense of truthfulness.

- The Moon and Sun are in sesqui-quadrate aspect, indicating tension between the transformative potential of the relationship and its reason for coming into being.
- Saturn and Pluto, which are in conjunction, surely challenge that harmony. Each of these planets is strong enough to overrule the expectation. Together, they pose a major threat.
- In addition, Mars is in square aspect to the Moon, indicating that if the relationship is to become more dynamic, the relationship has to have room for manoeuvre.

ii) The IC – the energy that the relationship relies upon for its own nourishment

The sign Virgo is on the IC, and Virgo's ruler Mercury is conjunct the MC and is the most elevated planet. This indicates the importance of practical, self-advancing values to the relationship's continuation. (Mark's father is a modern-day, self-made, hard-working man.) The inference is that both parties require their relationship to be supportive of the idea of moving on, whether that is seen in terms of social advancement or personal development. The sign Libra is intercepted in H4, indicating that there will be a change in the values that sustain the relationship. But even though the more relaxed, equable energy of Libra will eventually replace the energy of Virgo, Venus, the ruler of Libra, is in H 10 and keeps alive the connection with advancement.

- Mars in H7 is in exact trine to the IC and emphasises the theme of the relationship as an 'enabler'.

iii) Saturn – the area of challenge in the relationship

The presence of Saturn in Libra indicates that the major challenge to the relationship arises from problems of balance: between the two individuals concerned and also between the present reality and inherited expectations. This matter will come up again and again. In both instances, a lack of balance is likely to result in the relationship's being too concerned to meet expectations (Hannah, of her mother; Mark, of Hannah). This will be at the expense of authenticity. The placement of Saturn in H4 suggests that imbalances will manifest problems with the mothers and mothers' sides of the family, with properties, and with taking up opportunities overseas. At this stage, Hannah's and Mark's lives appear to be dominated by the perceived needs of Hannah's mother. Whilst not exactly expressing resentment, Mark is prepared to say that he thinks that Hannah's mother has a self-defeating value system – one that he does not underwrite. He would like them to have more space from her. Clearly, Hannah and Mark will have to make some conscious decisions about this overlap of their lives with Hannah's mother's life. Mark's own mother does not intrude into the relationship physically, but she is very much present because of the effect that her leaving her sons had on Mark, who now strives to please so as to avoid further rejection. It may be that in the interest of keeping the peace, Mark is concealing much dissatisfaction.

- Pluto is in very close conjunction to Saturn and will insist upon change introduced into the conventional structure of family. If this change does not come about as a result of conscious decision making, then Pluto will surely produce the disruption that will challenge the established order.

iv) The Part of Fortune – the raison d'être

With Pisces in H9, the Part of Fortune discloses that the desire to move out from the familiar is the raison d'être of the relationship. This 'moving out' may have a geographical or spiritual aspect.

For as long as this desire remains unacknowledged, both Hannah and Mark may be working against it and failing to recognise the point of their coming together.

As the Part of Fortune is exactly conjunct the Sun, the relationship is unlikely to thrive if moving out does not become part of Mark and Hannah's shared life.

4. Structuring the inquiry

Having collected the information, we can now answer the five questions:

1. To what will the relationship lend itself?

The relationship lends itself to a breaking free from conventional expectations and conditioned ideas, including the dominance of materialistic attitudes and values. It will encourage physical movement away from the familiar environment, perhaps to an overseas location. Indeed, such a development would make it easier for the relationship to fulfil its potential and open out the lives, sympathies, and awareness of the two parties involved.

2. What are the assumptions upon which the relationship was built, and to what extent will the relationship fulfil these assumptions?

The relationship has been built upon a desire to bring harmony into the lives of two young people who come from broken homes. Together, the two should move their lives into a more comfortable place whilst remaining closely connected to their families. The extent to which they will succeed in this is in direct relation to the willingness of both parties to break with the past and challenge the influence of their families, whose influence upon them is so strong that it threatens the authenticity of the relationship.

3.   What are its inner strengths and weaknesses?

The sesqui-quadrate between the Moon in H4 and the Sun in H9 indicates that the shift in expectation that is required to move the relationship on from its raison d'être is very considerable. In this matter, however, Saturn and Pluto support change. Jointly, they will bring about situations which will encourage conscious cooperation in the matter of challenging the hold that the past and conditioning have on the relationship. Saturn and Pluto are in trine aspect to the Sun and are therefore supportive of it.

Less supportive is Uranus, which is in square aspect to the Sun. If the pace of progress towards a greater separating out from the past/family and moving on is too slow, then Uranus will surely trigger, either ending the relationship or demanding a major review of priorities. The fact that Uranus is in trine aspect to Venus increases the chances of the relationship's surviving such a challenge.

4.   How does the relationship present itself to the world?

The relationship presents itself to the world as an affectionate, nurturing, harmonious partnership, but one which has arisen in response to difficult conditions within the families. Almost certainly, it will come to be seen as a cause of further trouble within those families because it is taking the two people concerned away from them.

5.   How do others respond to the relationship?

Others see the relationship as 'young' and, as a result, are inclined to interfere. Reclaiming their authority, steering their own affairs, and becoming more assertive are all lessons that the two people involved are invited to learn from being in this relationship.

Chapter 12

The Composite Chart and the Natal Charts – A Synastric Comparison

1. Introduction

In this chapter, we look at the practice of making a synastric comparison between the composite chart and the natal charts of the people involved. The point of such an exercise is to find out what each party makes of the relationship in which he or she is involved.

To undertake this exercise is to make compository even more labour-intensive than is already the case. Computer software cannot help us much here, other than to provide the natal charts of those involved. Still, this is a very rewarding exercise, one full of surprises (see endnote 1).

It is by no means the case that both parties are experiencing the same things from the relationship of which they are a part. Nor is it the case that they perceive the relationship in the same way. This is the exercise that is able to identify from where the problems are going to come. Obviously, however, the information is useful only inasmuch as those involved are receptive to what is disclosed. But if they are receptive, then this kind of analysis may put a name to and clarify things which hitherto a person has only been 'sort of aware of'.

Those who apply this technique to a relationship of their own will be well rewarded by what it is able to disclose.

2. The Technique

This technique requires the following:

- The natal charts of both parties
- The composite chart
- A synastric chart drawn up for each party against the composite chart

The quickest way to do this is to make, in turn, the birth chart of each individual the centre chart and then add, by hand, the luminaries, planets, hylegs, and key points from the composite chart.

Then, calculate the aspects as for any other synastric chart. See figures D and E.

From this, we can ascertain the way in which each party experiences the relationship. Again, this will create questions that will structure the inquiry.

For example:

1. To what extent is the purpose of the relationship (as defined in the previous section) compatible with the purpose of the individual?
2. To what extent does the relationship meet the relationship needs of the individual?
3. To what extent does it conform to the individual's assumptions about relationship?
4. What is the effect of the relationship upon the individual's Saturn problem?
5. To what extent does the relationship support Uranus in the creation of opportunity for the individual?

Obviously, this is not an exhaustive list. A student is encouraged to create his or her own questions based upon the kind of considerations that are of interest.

3. Finding the Answers to the Questions

1. To what extent is the purpose of the relationship (as defined in Chapter 3) compatible with the purpose of the individual?

Consider the following:

- the angular relationship between the Sun in the composite chart and the individual's chart, and the houses in which each falls
- house position/aspects formed between *inner* planets in the individual's chart and the composite Sun
- house position/aspects formed between *inner* planets in the composite chart and the Sun in the individual's chart
- house position/aspects formed between *outer* planets in the individual's chart and the Sun, *paying special attention to Saturn, the planet of restriction, and Uranus, the planet of opportunity.*
- house position/aspects formed between *outer* planets in the composite chart and the Sun in the individual's chart, *paying special attention to Saturn, the planet of restriction, and Uranus, the planet of opportunity.*

2. To what extent does the relationship meet the (intimate) relationship needs of the individual?

Consider the following:

- the sign on the cusp of H7 in the individual's chart (assess the extent to which the composite chart expresses this energy)

- the nature of the planets in the composite chart, if any, working through H7 of the individual's chart
- planets in the composite chart, if any, aspecting the Ascendant–Descendant axis in the individual's chart
- planets in the composite chart, if any, aspecting the Moon and Venus in the individual's chart

3. To what extent does it conform to the individual's assumptions about relationship?

Consider the extent to which the quality of the lunar energy in the individual's chart is expressed by the composite chart.

4. What is the effect of the relationship upon the individual's Saturn problem? Consider the following:

- aspects made by planets in the composite chart to Saturn in the individual's chart, *taking account of planetary strengths and the ability of Saturn in the individual's chart to dominate the inner planets/hylegs/ key points in the composite chart and the ability of the outer planets in the composite chart to challenge Saturn*
- the kind of energy that the composite chart sends into the house in which Saturn is found in the individual's chart

5. To what extent does the relationship support Uranus in the creation of opportunity for the individual?

Consider the following:

- the aspects made by composite Neptune and Pluto to Uranus in the individual's chart
- faster-moving aspects in the composite chart that Uranus may use as agents
- the energy sent by the composite chart into the area(s) of life (house[s]) in the individual's chart governed by Uranus
- the area of life (house) in the individual's chart into which composite Uranus sends it energy

We will now do this exercise using the chart of Hannah first, and then that of Mark.

4. Hannah and the Relationship

1. To what extent is the purpose of the relationship (as defined in the previous section) compatible with the purpose of the individual?

Consider the angular relationship between the Sun in the composite chart and the individual's chart, and the houses in which each falls.

The angular aspect between the composite Sun and the Sun of Hannah is a semi-square. The tension of this placement is accentuated by the fact that the two suns occupy adjacent houses: one a fire house; the other, a water house. This amounts to a lack of compatibility between the purpose of the relationship and Hannah's own purpose, but, obviously, the degree of incompatibility is less than would be the case if the aspect involved were a square or an opposition. Even so, this aspect will make it relatively difficult for Hannah to readily appreciate what the relationship is able to do for her and Mark. The young person with the Sun in H8, which, of course, is a water house, usually has a passive approach to emotive situations and rarely expects to be the one to introduce change. Hannah does, however, have inner planets, including Mars, in H9, which offsets this passivity to some degree.

The fact that composite Sun and composite Mercury both fall in Hannah's H7 indicates that her consciousness is receptive to the idea that the challenges that the relationship brings are a legitimate aspect of being in a relationship.

Hannah's Sun falls in H10 of the composite chart and indicates that Hannah's conscious contribution is to encourage the relationship to have structure and status in the eyes of others, as she sees this as being the way to get the best out of the relationship.

Aspects formed between inner planets in the individual's chart and the composite Sun: none.

Aspects formed between inner planets in the composite chart and the Sun in the individual's chart: Squaring Hannah's Sun is composite Mars in Capricorn in H7. Mars in H7 looks to others to bring in energy, incentive, and direction; in Capricorn, it attracts personalities in whom the Capricornian vibration is strong.

Composite Mars expresses itself through H5 in Hannah's chart and indicates that this involvement of other people challenges Hannah to focus upon her creative potential, including her ability to have children. This kind of focus upon self does not come easily to a person with the Sun in H8 who expects to fit in with others.

Consider the house position/aspects formed between outer planets in the individual's chart and the Sun, paying special attention to Saturn, the planet of restriction, and Uranus, the planet of opportunity.

Although Hannah's Saturn makes no aspect to the composite Sun, her Uranus is in square aspect to it. Hannah's Uranus will trigger if the relationship is cramping her in the house occupied by her Uranus. This is H4, which is also the house in which composite Uranus falls.

Hannah's Uranus falls in H5 of the composite chart. This is a major clue as to who is likely to be the partner engaging in extramarital affairs which threaten to disrupt the relationship.

Consider the house position/aspects formed between outer planets in the composite chart and the Sun in the individual's chart, paying special attention to Saturn, the planet of restriction, and Uranus, the planet of opportunity.

Composite Saturn and Pluto make an opposition aspect to Hannah's Sun from H3. Although, technically, it is just out of orbs, the fact that two planets are involved – two planets, moreover, that are both significantly slower than the Sun – means that this aspect should be taken into consideration. It will be noted that Hannah's Saturn and Pluto are already in this house, and so this influence from the composite chart simply reinforces a theme with which Hannah is already struggling: that of the restricting the effect of family and environment and the developmental requirement to separate out.

Summary

Although the relationship will act as an agent of change in her life, especially through the influence of Pluto, it does not seem as though Hannah is able to engage with this idea in any meaningful way. Its presence in her life will simply exacerbate existing tensions with the family without providing her with much that will inspire her to do this positively or purposefully. She accepts the challenges as part of being in a relationship rather than engaging with them in any creative way.

2. To what extent does the relationship meet the (intimate) relationship needs of the individual?

Consider the sign on the cusp of H7 in the individual's chart and assess the extent to which the composite chart expresses this energy.

The sign Pisces is on the cusp of Hannah's H7. This indicates the energy that she needs to bring into her life to balance out her Virgoan consciousness.

Mark himself does not have Pisces represented in his energetic profile, but the composite chart does: composite Sun and composite Mercury are both in Pisces, which means that the relationship is able to provide Hannah with the more spacious, flexible perspectives she needs. She will view this positively, even though it will challenge the tidy view of life perceived through her Virgoan Ascendant.

Consider the nature of the planets in the composite chart, if any, working through H7 of the individual's chart.

Both composite Sun and composite Mercury are working through Hannah's H7. This means that she will identify the relationship with the Piscean energy and consciously acknowledge that the relationship brings into her life a different way of being and seeing.

Consider planets in the composite chart, if any, aspecting the Ascendant–Descendant axis in the individual's chart.

Composite Venus, Mars, Saturn, and Neptune all make harmonious aspects to Hannah's Ascendant–Descendant axis, whilst the Sun is conjunct to the Descendant. This indicates the scale of Hannah's emotional involvement in the relationship and undoubtedly accounts for the impression of harmony and compatibility that she and Mark give out when they are together. She views the relationship as complementary to herself as an individual.

Consider planets in the composite chart, if any, aspecting the Moon and Venus in the individual's chart, taking into account the house placements of Moon and Venus in the composite chart and the houses through which they work in the individual's chart.

Composite Venus and composite Jupiter both make sextiles to Hannah's Moon. These are emotionally soothing aspects. Composite Mars trines Hannah's Venus, which, too, is complementary energy and indicates that she feels at ease with the expressive aspects of the relationship, including the physical relationship.

Composite Chiron is exactly conjunct Hannah's Venus in H10, emphasising a theme in her natal chart: love will be an agent in the Chironic process of making Hannah grow up and take responsibility for the direction of her own life.

Summary

The abundance of harmonious aspects to the emotionally sensitive points in Hannah's chart indicates that both emotionally and physically, the relationship does meet her requirements of an intimate relationship very well, indeed.

3. To what extent does it conform to the individual's assumptions about relationship?

Consider the extent to which the quality of the lunar energy in the individual's chart is expressed by the composite chart.

Hannah's Moon in Capricorn on the cusp of H5 and H6 indicates that her assumption about relationship focuses upon the relationship's ability to provide material security. She will expect the partner to be sober, responsible, and, in some way, senior to her.

In the composite chart, the Capricornian theme is picked up by Mercury on the cusp of H9 and H10, Venus in H10, and Mars in the sign Capricorn. Within the relationship, these planets will produce a focus compatible with Hannah's expectations. Mercury and Venus indicate that, within the relationship, energy goes into building an aspirational lifestyle, whilst Mars, as noted earlier, indicates that Hannah and Mark bring into their lives people with Capricornian attitudes and values.

The challenge to Hannah's expectations comes from composite Pluto in Libra, but, as noted earlier, this emphasises an existing theme in Hannah's chart rather than introduces anything new.

4. What is the effect of the relationship upon the individual's Saturn problem?

Consider aspects made by planets in the composite chart to Saturn in the individual's chart, taking account of planetary strengths and the ability of Saturn in the individual's chart to dominate the inner planets/hylegs/key points in the composite chart and the ability of the outer planets in the composite chart to challenge Saturn.

The first thing to note about composite Saturn is that it is in exact conjunction to composite Pluto. Whilst this will add intensity to Saturnian issues, it will ensure that those issues are transformative. When Saturn stands alone, there is no such guarantee.

In Hannah's natal chart, Saturn and Pluto are also conjunct, and so the influence from the composite chart adds weight by making the relationship the agent of the transformative situations.

The fact that composite Pluto rules H5 indicates that it is working through a consciousness, shared by Hannah and Mark, that, for all of its heavy conditioning by family, is, in the final analysis, individualistic and will do what it wants to do. In Hannah's case, issues brought about by the relationship have been instrumental in bringing out this aspect in her life, hence the problems with the family, especially her mother.

Composite Saturn, the ruler of Capricorn, makes harmonious but subduing aspects to Hannah's Ascendant–Descendant, as does her natal Saturn. It intensifies the opposition aspect in Hannah's chart between natal Mercury and natal Saturn, which describes the conflict that she experiences between wanting to move her life on and have new experiences and yet not wanting to break with the family and the familiar way of being. But the fact that Pluto is behind Saturn means that this conflict will be transformative and, in time, will encourage Mercury in H9 to function more freely.

Consider the kind of energy that the composite chart sends into the house in which Saturn is found in the individual's chart.

This is covered above.

5. To what extent does the relationship support Uranus in the creation of opportunity for the individual?

Aspects made by composite Neptune and Pluto to Uranus in the individual's chart: none.

Consider faster-moving aspects in the composite chart that Uranus may use as agents.

In Hannah's chart, composite Uranus is conjunct Jupiter, which rules H7 and H8 and which signifies that relationships will be the principal agent used by Uranus in its task of freeing Hannah from limitation. The effect of her relationships, particularly those involving intimacy, will be to increase Hannah's awareness of her options and opportunities as a woman.

The energy sent by the composite chart into the area(s) of life (house[s]) in the individual's chart governed (accidentally) by Uranus: none.

Consider the area of life (house) in the individual's chart into which composite Uranus sends it energy.

In Hannah's chart, composite Uranus is working through the same house that is occupied by her natal Uranus. If her relationship were with someone significantly older, then composite Uranus could send its energy into another house, thereby creating an additional conduit for Uranian energy. As it is, it is reinforcing the weight of natal Uranus, which, in Hannah's chart, is conjunct Jupiter, which rules H7 and H8 and which signifies that relationships will be the principal agent used by Uranus in its task of freeing Hannah from limitation. The effect of her relationships, particularly those involving intimacy, will be to increase Hannah's awareness of her options and opportunities as a woman.

It must be assumed, therefore, that Hannah's relationship with Mark is serving this purpose and is giving her confidence in her femininity. But, because Uranus shadows Jupiter in both the natal and composite chart, the relationship itself will be challenged by the very process it is encouraging.

Summary

The composite chart only emphasises the message of natal Uranus. It does not add any new dimensions.

Conclusion: Hannah and the Composite Chart

For Hannah, her relationship with Mark is something that appeals to her emotionally and physically, but it does not appear to be making it any easier for her to understand her developmental need to become more independent of her family. Indeed, she is likely to have experienced the situation as having become more uncomfortable since Mark has been in the picture. She accepts this forbearance rather than having any sense that, for her, the relationship could be a way on.

5. Mark and the Relationship

1. To what extent is the purpose of the relationship compatible with the purpose of the individual?

Consider the angular relationship between the Sun in the composite chart and the individual's chart, and the houses in which each falls.

As is the case with Hannah's Sun, Mark's Sun and the Sun of the composite chart are in semi-square aspect to each other and involve adjacent houses. Mark's Sun, although technically in H9, sends its influence into H10. The comments made regarding Hannah's Sun apply here, also.

Consider the house position/aspects formed between inner planets in the individual's chart and the composite Sun.

In Mark's chart, Mercury makes a semi-sextile. The Moon and Jupiter both make trines to the composite Sun, which indicates that Mark is able to engage both intellectually and emotionally with the purpose of the relationship – which is to move both parties on in their understanding. That means that he will be more comfortable than Hannah with the discomforts and disruptions caused by their relationship.

Consider the house position/aspects formed between inner planets in the composite chart and the Sun in the individual's chart.

Although the composite Moon makes a square aspect to Mark's Sun – and we will need to consider the significance of this in later sections of this inquiry – composite Mercury and composite Chiron both make harmonious aspects to Mark's Sun. The conjunction from composite Mars is particularly powerful, involving as it does his MC, as well. All of these connections have the power to help move on Mark's life by broadening his social sphere and increasing his incentive to go somewhere with his life. In this respect, composite Mars is particularly significant. Located in H7 in the composite chart and ruling H5 and H10, it indicates that Mark as an individual has been both energised and assisted by the relationship itself and by the personalities that have come into his life since he has been with Hannah. In this, we must include Hannah's parents, who are materially ambitious.

Consider the house position/aspects formed between outer planets in the individual's chart and the Sun, paying special attention to Saturn, the planet of restriction, and Uranus, the planet of opportunity.

With respect to the composite Sun and Mark's outer planets, the situation is less harmonious. Composite Uranus is aligned with his natal Uranus, which is square to the composite Sun. As noted in Hannah's inquiry, it is a seriously destabilising factor. Although technically out of orbs, Mark's natal Pluto is in quincunx aspect to composite Sun. As natal Pluto is reinforced by composite Pluto, this aspect should be considered. The story here is that Mark's own developmental process, which requires him to balance out the amount of time and energy that goes into his relationships, will almost certainly put the relationship with Hannah, for all that it is able to encourage growth, under considerable strain. But, of course, when a person has a need to become freer from reliance upon relationship, this state of affairs is a form of opportunity.

House position/aspects formed between outer planets in the composite chart and the Sun in the individual's chart, paying special attention to Saturn, the planet of restriction, and Uranus, the planet of opportunity: none.

Summary

The number of harmonious mutual contacts between Mark's Sun and inner planets and the composite Sun and inner planets indicate that Mark is able to engage consciously with the purpose of the relationship and to cooperate with it. But whether it will encourage him to become more conscious of his need to put more energy into his own life and direction remains to be seen. The future health of the relationship depends upon his achieving a better balance. Until then, it is under threat from the workings of his outer planets.

2. To what extent does the relationship meet the (intimate) relationship needs of the individual?

Consider the sign on the cusp of H7 in the individual's chart and assess the extent to which the composite chart expresses this energy.

In Mark's case, the sign Scorpio occupies the Descendant, indicating that this is the energy he needs to balance out his Taurean Ascendant.

Although the composite chart does not have a pronounced Scorpio theme, Jupiter, which is in Scorpio in the composite chart, falls in Mark's House of Relationship and provides the energy he requires. Composite Jupiter rules H6 and H9 in the composite chart and identifies these areas of life as ones in which the relationship can encourage a more expansive attitude.

Consider the nature of the planets in the composite chart, if any, and work through H7 of the individual's chart. (See above.)

Consider planets in the composite chart, if any, aspecting the Ascendant–Descendant axis in the individual's chart.

In Mark's chart, composite Mercury is sextile to his Ascendant (and, therefore, trine the Descendant). The Moon, which is quincunx his Ascendant, will make a semi-sextile to the Descendant. Both these aspects promote ease of exchange between two people.

Composite Chiron, which falls in Marks H1, reinforcing natal Chiron, is, however, a reminder of Mark's developmental need to find a better balance between himself as an individual and his relationships.

Consider planets in the composite chart, if any, aspecting the Moon and Venus in the individual's chart.

Composite Venus is in square aspect to Mark's Moon, and Neptune is in opposition. These aspects indicate a conflict in the values and focus of the relationship and those of Mark's emotional self. His natal Moon in Gemini in H2 and H3 describes a cerebral way of interacting, which the relationship challenges. And, because Saturn and Pluto both aspect Mark's Moon, we must assume that his own emotional expectations are being changed by the relationship, although this is sure to be a source of discomfort for him. Although Saturn and Pluto both make trine aspects, no contact from these planets is experienced lightly.

Composite Uranus, in sextile aspect to Mark's Venus, *does,* however, lighten a person's emotional interactions and makes them stimulating.

Summary

Mark's emotional needs are less well met by the relationship than Hannah's, but even so, there is enough nourishment – perhaps too much – to make the relationship a threat to Mark's efforts to become a stronger, more confident individual.

3. To what extent does it conform to the individual's assumptions about relationship?

Consider the extent to which the quality of the lunar energy in the individual's chart is expressed by the composite chart.

Geminian energy forms no part of the make-up of the relationship, but composite Mercury (in Pisces) is the most elevated planet, sending its energy into H10 and encouraging rational involvement in the matter of constructing an aspirational lifestyle. Additionally, the Moon and Saturn are both in Libra, which will make the relationship one in which consideration and other-regardingness are factors. As Pluto shadows both these planets, however, the lightness and freedom from intensity which Mark, with his Moon in Gemini, likes to experience in his relationships is surely missing.

4. What is the effect of the relationship upon the individual's Saturn problem?

Consider aspects made by planets in the composite chart to Saturn in the individual's chart, taking account of planetary strengths and the ability of Saturn in the individual's chart to dominate the inner planets/hylegs/key points in the composite chart and the ability of the outer planets in the composite chart to challenge Saturn.

The exact conjunction of Saturn and Pluto in the composite chart, aligning itself as it does with Mark's Saturn/Pluto/Part of Fortune conjunction, gives the theme of transformation of consciousness through relationship a relentless intensity, throwing up again and again situations with which Mark is required to deal consciously.

Without much prior experience of relationship, Mark almost certainly assumes that this is what being in a relationship does. To a degree, he is correct. But later in his life, if he has other relationship experiences, especially with people from a different age group, he may find that the buttons are not always pressed quite so hard.

The exact sextile from composite Neptune will increase the difficulty that Mark, a Saturn-in-Libra person, will have in remaining clear about boundaries.

Consider the kind of energy that the composite chart sends into the house in which Saturn is found in the individual's chart.

In addition to the energy of Saturn and Pluto, described above, the composite Moon in Libra is also present in Mark's H6. As we know, the Moon does not give out energy, but it will attract and focus the energy of planets that it aspects. Of these, Saturn is the most powerful, but Mark's Sun in Capricorn is also involved.

The Moon in Libra, when working through H6, may, in its anxiety to please and keep the peace, behave in a passive, servile way. Mark's need to keep Hannah happy, and Hannah's materialism and conditioning to be a hard worker, will encourage him to play safer in respect to his work and future than he would do if he were alone. Given Mark's developmental requirement, this is obviously not beneficial.

5. 5. To what extent does the relationship support Uranus in the creation of opportunity for the individual?

Aspects made by composite Neptune and Pluto to Uranus in the individual's chart: none.

Consider faster-moving aspects in the composite chart that Uranus may use as agents.

Mark's Uranus in Sagittarius is in square aspect to the composite Sun in Pisces, which indicates that Mark's own need to be more authentic and freer in his relationship will, to some degree, express itself through the inclusive energy and perspectives of Pisces.

Consider the energy sent by the composite chart into the area(s) of life (house[s]) in the individual's chart governed by Uranus.

In Mark's chart, Uranus governs H11 and weaves fellowship into the theme of liberation. Composite Sun, Mercury, and Venus indicate that the relationship will broaden Mark's social sphere, putting him in touch with people with more philosophical ideas and reducing his reliance upon the company of Hannah alone.

Consider the area of life (house) in the individual's chart into which composite Uranus sends it energy.

Composite Uranus sends its energy into Mark's H7. In a wide conjunction aspect with Jupiter, this influence emphasises the theme of liberation. Jupiter's influence and the fact that both of these planets have a connection to composite H5 make this imperative more attractive and more connected to the idea of building individuality.

Summary

The composite chart emphasises the message of natal Uranus, but it also introduces a new dimension in the form of friendships that are likely to encourage Mark to broaden his ideas.

Conclusion: Mark and the Relationship

The synastric comparison suggests that, in the relationship, Mark is more responsive than Hannah to the challenges that the relationship throws up. Although emotionally it is less comfortable for him than it is for Hannah, Mark is able to feel stimulated by the newness that the relationship is bringing into his life. This could make a significant contribution to his eventually questioning some very basic assumptions that he has had about relationship and his responsibilities to meet the expectations of others. For Mark, the relationship is a more transformative experience than for Hannah, whose basic assumptions are not seriously challenged by it.

Endnote

1. Students will have to decide for themselves whether hard work involved in a synastric comparison between an individual and the composite chart is worth the effort. That assessment may be better made when the exercise has been applied to a relationship situation that would benefit from some insight and clarity. For sure, there are few other methods of analysis from within or from outside the world of astrology that yield up the inside story on a relationship in the way that this technique is able to provide.

Appendix: Timing in Compository

This exercise requires a familiarity with time-working techniques.

A composite chart is a contrivance inasmuch as it reflects no moment in time, as is the case for a birth.

This means that the practice of progressing the chart, using the ephemeris and the idea that a day of life corresponds to a year of life, is not applicable.

There is, however, a simple way of getting an idea of timing: using a method that is derived from a technique based upon the axial rotation of the Earth. Properly done, this technique takes into account a planet's declination. The calculation is done using trigonometry.

The method that I recommend here is a simplification, involving neither declination nor trigonometry. It assumes that the following are true:

- One day equals one year.
- Each planet, as ruler of a house, is a significator of an area of life.
- A planet will be carried to the position occupied by a planet farther ahead of it in the zodiac by the axial rotation of the Earth, which moves the house at a rate of one degree every four minutes in a clockwise motion, putting a new degree on the MC. This is called a converse direction. It means, in effect, that any planet may advance on any other, regardless of the relative speeds, because, according to this method, they are being moved by the illusion created by the motion of the Earth, not by their own motion.
- The planet which is farther ahead is considered to be held stationary whilst the other planet advances on it.
- A planet may advance on a planet with which it has no aspect.

No matter how crude this method may seem, it will yield significant results.

Method

1. Consider each planet in the chart, and note the area of life that is signifies.

For example, in the composite chart of Hannah and Mark, Mars in H7 is the ruler of H5 (creativity/sexuality) and H 10 (lifestyle).

When this planet comes together with Jupiter, Jupiter can be expected to give a helpful boost to Mars, the significator of sexuality, creativity, and lifestyle.

In the composite chart, Mars and Jupiter are in sextile aspect, with an orb of influence of 3 degrees. In three years, therefore, Mars will be carried to make an exact sextile to Jupiter. This will impact favourably upon Mars and the things it signifies.

When Mars comes together with Saturn, the slower-moving planet will dominate. It is to be expected that the Martian drive through H7, which gives the relationship much of its point, will be subdued.

In the composite chart, these two planets are in wide square aspect, with an orb of influence of 7 degrees. As Mars is behind Saturn, in seven years Mars will be carried by a converse direction into exact square aspect with Saturn. Difficulties in the relationship are to be expected.

2. Use the table of aspects drawn up at the time of constructing the composite chart to identify the contacts and establish timings in connection with the most significant aspects. For example:

Sun is in square aspect to Uranus with an orb of influence of 3 degrees. This means that after three years, the relationship will have experienced a major challenge. Clearly, it has come through. But it is to be noted that this would have occurred at the same time when Jupiter was making contact to Mars, indicating that the relationship changed gears at that time and, for a while, at least, destabilised itself.

3. Be aware of the effects of Saturn and the outer planets. As they are carried or planets are carried to them in order to make exact aspects to significant and sensitive points in the composite chart, they will challenge its integrity.

Postscript

Early in 2004, after having been together for eight years, Hannah and Mark split. Hannah says that she was tired of Mark's increasingly negative attitude towards her mother. It is also the case that Hannah met someone else who looks remarkably like Mark, only less athletic. She met him in a club when she was at a colleague's leaving party, shortly after Mark told her that he was not yet ready to get married. She and Mark split about a month later.

Mark is saying nothing. He has not got anyone else. He has moved back in with his father and is spending his time with friends from the running club.

How seriously is this split to be taken? It occurred after transiting Uranus passed over Hannah's descendant (Mark declined to get married). Immediately afterwards, it made a conjunction to the Sun in the composite chart (Hannah took herself out with the women at work for the first time ever). Straight after that, it made a square to Mark's Uranus in H7 (Mark found out about Hannah's new boyfriend and moved out).

As far as Hannah is concerned, the split is final. She and her new partner will be getting engaged shortly. But she speaks as one who just has to keep going forwards because she cannot bear to look back. Between Hannah and her new man, there appears to be nothing of the rapport that existed between her and Mark.

It appears that Mark's slowness in committing to family life made Hannah feel more vulnerable than she admitted to feeling. It is not without significance that the new young man says that the thing he most wants is to get married and have a family.

Then, in the summer of 2004, Hannah and Mark got back together. They are now considering the possibility of moving to New Zealand because they both feel cramped in Brighton. They are increasingly aware that living at too close a range to their troubled families may not be such a good idea, after all. 'Moving out' now appears to be on the cards.

Update, 2014

Ten years on, friends of Hannah's family report that Hannah and Mark are in Melbourne, Australia. They have three children: two boys and a girl. Now the elder children are settled in school, and Mark's work is paying well since he added coaching to fitness instruction, the family have no plans to return to England. They have moved on. We can only guess at what it cost them and their parents, but as a couple, they took the measures that saved their own relationship. They intend to marry, in Melbourne, in four years time, on Hannah's thirty-fifth birthday, and are hoping that both sets of parents will be there.